LABOUR ECONOMICS AND LABOUR PROBLEMS

M.V. JOSHI

ATLANTIC
PUBLISHERS & DISTRIBUTORS (P) LTD

ATLANTIC
PUBLISHERS & DISTRIBUTORS (P) LTD

7/22, Ansari Road, Darya Ganj, New Delhi
Tel.: +91-11-4077 5252, 2327 3880
E-mail: orders@atlanticbooks.com
Web: www.atlanticbooks.com

Reprint 2026

Published by Atlantic Publishers & Distributors (P) Ltd.

Printed & bound in India by Atlantic Print Services

Preface

Labour Economics and Labour Problems is an integral part of mainstream Economics. But its crucial importance gives it the status of a separate independent subject. After new economic reforms, labour problems drew attention of the Government, researchers and writers.

This book has been prepared according to syllabi prescribed in Economics, Commerce and Labour at graduate and post-graduate level. It analyses the wage theories, labour market, migration, wage issues and wage policy, turnover and absentism, child labour, female labour, unorganised labour and labour problems of new economic reforms. This book will be very useful to the students, teachers and researchers.

I am very thankful to Prof. A.L. Patel for his kind help in writing this book. I am also thanksful to Mrs. Usha M. Joshi for her generous support.

I want to convey my special thanks to Dr. K.R. Gupta and M/s Atlantic Publishers and Distributors, New Delhi for agreeing to publish this book expeditiously.

M.V. JOSHI

CONTENTS

1

Theories of Wages — 1

"So long as workers are not guaranteed sufficient and reasonable wages, neither industrial peace nor workers satisfaction with the job is possible."

—*Ram Avtar*

Outline of the Chapter

1. Introduction.
2. Characteristic of Wages.
3. Importance of Wages.
4. Theories of Wages.
   (i) Subsistence Theory
   (ii) Standard of living Theory
   (iii) Wages Fund Theory
   (iv) Residual Claimant Theory
   (v) Karl Marx's Theory of Exploitation

1. Introduction

Meaning of Wages. "Labour" is a human-ability of human-power, which is projected to any type of physical, mental or combination of both the work. The main aim of this work is to get the income. Whatever monetary, economic benefits (financial) the person who works (labourer) gets for doing this type of work is called "Wages" in economical term. There are different types of wages, *viz.* wages according to work (work, related wages), time-related wages, monetary wages, real wages etc. But in economics mainly monetary wage is discussed. So we can say that whatever monetary income non-monetary benefits a person gets for his physical or mental work is called "Wages".

2. Characteristics of Wages

It is essential to know, some important characteristics or features of wages, to understand its concept clearly. "Wages" is a broad and deep concept. It is widely interpreted. Many aspects and views are waved around it. Its main feature or characteristics are says following...

1. A person gets wages for physical or mental or both types labour work.
2. This Labour work is mainly production-oriented. Wage is given for any labour used for production of any thing or services.
3. Wage can be in the form of monetary income or in the form of non-monetary benefits. *i.e.* in cash or kind. In other words, wages include monetary (financial) wages and non-monetary benefits *i.e.* accommodation, food, health, touring, entertainment and other facilities.
4. There are certain concepts, principles and standards for determining the wages. According to these standards wages are fixed or changed.
5. Wage is given for certain time limit such as hours, days, weeks, monthly, half yearly or yearly or subject to some work or by work.
6. Wages differ according to different industries, profession, area or region. It also differs, according to type and class of the laboureres. There are differences in wages according to seasons and time factor. Thus, various varieties and differences can be observed in large number in wage framework.
7. Wage is given in return of sale of labour but not for sell of labourers. Labour cannot be separated from the labourer as a tool of production. So presence of labourer is inevitable when and where labour is needed. Presence of labourer raises certain problems, at the place of production.
8. As the labour is an element, attached with the labourer (means a person) only economic calculations are not taken for consideration for fixing wages. Human, social etc. factors are also considered for fixing the wages.
9. Wages does not depend only on the matters such as demand of labour and supply of labour but life style, relative bargaining power, political interference etc.
10. There are various modes of wage payment; such as time based payment, result-oriented payment, efficiency based payment, premium, bonus system etc.
11. Wage is the main source (factor) of income for labourers. Hence, wage is the prime factor determining the living standard of labourer.
12. Wage is the main factor in total cost of production. Proportion of wages in total production cost depends on whether the production

system is labour-oriented or capital-oriented and on the type of production. Proportion of wages in total production cost is more remarkable in labour based and primitive production system. While it is very less in capital-oriented and modern production system.

3. Importance of Wages

Discussion of wages and wage problems are not important only in labour economics but it is also important for industrial system and in context of economy. In the concept of wages, there are differences between owners and labourers. For producers wages is an expense. So they are not willing (ready) to give wage according to the demand of labourers, while on other side, for labourers wage is the main source of income. So it is natural that they may wish to get maximum wage. Thus, the Aptitude (approach) of owners and labourers are contradictory in the matter of giving wage and taking wage. But continuation of low wage, for a long time is not advisable for the interest of the society. Besides this, policy of low wage is not proper in context with labourers efficiency, productivity and living standard. "So long as workers are not guaranteed sufficient and reasonable wages, neither industrial peace nor worker's satisfaction with the job is possible."[1]

Karl Marks has said that problem of wages is not merely economic problem, but it is social and political problem; because, wage rate affects to the labourer's standard of living. Lower rate of wages create economic inequality in society and it causes possibilities of social tension and friction. When number of labourers are large, they can affect national politics (particularly in democracy) and hence, politics also gets affected. Political interference is observed in fixing the wages. Exploitation of labourers, due to low wages and linking wages with politics and economic system, would demolish capitalism and socialism shall be established.

4. Theories of wages

"Thoughts and theories regarding how much wages should be given to the labourers; why and how these wages is decided etc., matter are called theories of wages." Many principles have been represented by various economists at different times regarding wages. These principles were put by classical economists, neo-classical economists and modern economists.

First of all in important theories of wages, subsistence theory was given by Malthus etc. represented about it. Then after Ricardo represented standard of living theory. Karl Marx represented theory of exploitation on the basis of surplus value. Adam Smith, Jevons and Walker put the theory of Residual Claimant. J.S. Mill represented wage fund theory.

Modern economists represented theories such as demand and supply theory, marginal productivity theory and theory of collective bargaining. For this concept of fair wage and minimum wage is being represented.

According to modern concepts, the labourers should be participated in management and they should also get the share from the profit (means bonus) besides their pay *i.e.*, wage.

Thus, we can clearly observe continuous change coming in the concept of wages and approaches of theories and thinking. Now, let's discuss differently about the main principles of wages.

(i) Subsistence Theory

(A) *Representation and Explanation* :

According to this theory, a labourer should be given a minimum living wage or wage sufficient for his existence. Philosophers of France and mercantilists of Britain represented their thoughts between 1630 to 1775.

Malthus's Principle of population is attached with it. According to it, labourer should be given a minimum living wage only. To maintain the equal balance of population and hence, of the labourers it is recommended to give the labourers a minimum living wage.

If labourers would be given higher wages than their requirements, they will marry at early age. So population and as a result proportion of labourer would increase and wages shall decrease. Contrary to this, if wages would be lower than requirement, the proportion of marriage would decrease. Infant mortality rate would increase and thus the supply of labourers would decrease and wages would increase. So it was represented that to balance, the population and rate of wages, labourers should be given a minimum living wage.

(B) *Peculiarities of the Theory* :

1. Merchantalists believed that to keep export commodity's price low, a minimum living wage is to be given to the labourers attached with production. Thus, export would increase and proportion of Silver and Gold would increase. More benefits would be there due to trade.
2. This theory is also linked with the cost of commodity. According to it, the cost of the commodity depends on labour-cost. Low wages would decrease the cost and high wages would increase the cost.
3. This theory was very important during the preliminary stage of industrial development.

4. The economists of Germany called this theory as an "Iron Law of Wages."
5. This theory is based on two convictions. In agriculture law of diminishing return is observed, so in agricultural produce, more growth cannot be achieved. And population increases at higher rate.
6. This theory spread widely in West Europe during 18th century and in the beginning of 19th century, when population increased at higher rate, while production of crop didn't increase that much. This theory was widely supported after publication of Malthus's "Essay on Population."
7. According to this theory, labour power is a commodity which is being sold by labourers to owner. In long term, cost of labour becomes equals to its expense.

(C) *Drawbacks of the Doctrine* :

1. This doctrine thinks about supply of labour only. It has not thought about demand of labour.
2. It cannot be accepted in any reference that labourers should be given wages only equal to living wage.
3. Today labour union activities have developed much. Their activities largely effects the wages. But in this theory, it has not been noted.
4. The belief that labourers would be lazy and they would marry at early age, if they get more wage than living wage is not logical.
5. In this law, the possible adverse effects of low wages have not marked.
6. No discussion regarding wage differences have been done in this theory.
7. It has not clarified how and which matters would be included in "life wage"/"subsistence".
8. This law explains about long term wage scale. But it is unable to explain current market wage scale prevailing at certain time.
9. This is a pessimist theory in which it's stated that labourers have no future. No optimism is put forward that condition of labourers shall improve due to their efficiency or due to improvement in economic condition.
10. Efficiency of the labourers is neglected and it is not marked anywhere that a labourer's wage shall increase, along with his efficiency.
11. This principle is based on Malthus's principle of population. Malthus's principle of population has been highly criticised and it's irrelevant in present context.

12. It is a wrong belief that supply of labourers will increase due to increase in wage.
13. According to this theory, the wages of a particular certain place's labourers should be equal, as their living standard is also equal. But in practical life, different wage is observed, for different type of labourers in the same profession.
14. This doctrine is not proper by moral, social and even human outlook. It's not righteous to give same wage to the labourer whether the labourer is skilled or unskilled. Same way it's not judicious to give wages, which is just sufficient only to sustain his life.

(ii) Standard of Living Theory

(A) *Representation and Explanation* :

According to this theory labourer should get wage sufficient to maintain living standard, and not equal to living (life) wage.

Living standard is a broad concept. To understand the concept of living standard, it is necessary that factors like classification of per capita expense, satisfaction of various needs etc. must be taken into account. Concept of living standard can be understood by possession of per head facility. We can say that living standard is high, if one gets facility of education, hygiene and entertainment, besides getting full primary needs. Thus, from this discussion, it can be said that concept of living standard is totally different than that of living (life) wage.

According to Ricardo, natural wage rate does not remain steady but it varies. Wage rate varies according to change in living standard and condition of life. Wage rate increases as needs of labourers increase.

(B) *Peculiarities* :

1. According to this doctrine, efficiency is taken into account in wages, and so it is believed that wage would be more than subsistence.
2. While determining wage, only inevitable needs are not considered, but needs of education, hygiene, entertainment etc. are also being considered in this doctrine.
3. According to this doctrine, wages should be such that the labourer should be able to maintain their due living standard. If the wage is less than it, the supply of labourers would decrease and if more wage is given, the supply of labourer would increase.
4. In this theory, labourer's efficiency has been noted. Here labourer's efficiency has been noted. Here it is said that, if a labourer gets wages according to his living standard; their productivity would increase.

5. A labourer would be habituated to high living standard, if he is given high wage, for remarkable time. Hence, he shall work more to retain his level, or he would increase his efficiency. For this he would marry late or keep his family's size limited.
6. If labourer would get more wage than subsistence wage, he shall spare for the future and he shall be able to fight for more wage.
7. If economic development is fast, demand of labourers will be more than its supply. Hence, wages will be high and their living standard would go high. So, their population would increase. As a result, supply of labourers would increase than demand, and again, wages shall be low. Thus, the labourer's wages would be determined on the basis of their living standard.

(C) *Defects or Limitations or Drawbacks* :

1. The labourers are not habituated with certain living standards. Person's living standard is not fixed.
2. Wage cannot be increased more than its marginal productivity even if wage is based on living standard.
3. In this theory, demand of labour is not taken into account. Only concept of supply of labour have been considered.
4. Concept of living standard is not specific, steady or clear. It is variable, indefinite and vague.
5. Here it is said that, wage is based on living standard, but in fact base of living standard is dependent on wage. It is impossible to improve living standard, without increasing wage.
6. If we think that, wage should be fixed according to living standard, then a person's living standard does not change for a certain period. It means that there should be no change in wage. Actually, wage changes frequently.
7. Living standard indirectly effects demand and supply of labour, while demand and supply of labour directly effects wages.

(iii) Wages Fund Theory

First of all, J.S. Mill, represented this theory systematically. According to it, wage depends on available capital fund for it, which is known as Wage Fund. Two prime factors effects wage fund— proportion of population and available capital for wage payment. If labour Force increases due to increase in population and wage fund remains constant, then wage decreases. Contrary to it if labour force decreases, wage increases. Similarly if labour force does not change, but if wage fund increases, then wage increases. And if wage fund decreases, wage also decreases.

"The theory briefly states that wages depends on the proportion between population and capital, or rather between the number of labouring classes who work for return and the aggregate of what can be called the wages fund which consists of that part of circulating capital which is expended in the direct return of labour."

According to J.S. Mill, every owner keeps provision of fixed capital; for wages of labourers, which is called as wage fund. This fund is constant and mostly non-convertible. So wage is based on labour force. If labour force increases wage decreases and if it decreases there is increase in wage.

Wage increases only if either wage fund increases or number of labourers decreases. Under the impression of Malthus, Mill states that due to continuous growth in population, wage shall decrease. So to maintain wage level it is inevitable that labourers must keep their family size limited.

(A) *Characteristics of the Theory* :

1. This concept (theory) is superior to the theory of subsistence and theory of living standard.
2. We can't say that, it is one-sided or partial, because in this theory demands of labour and supply of labour both are given equal importance. In fact, theory of wage fund can be said balanced and well proportionate, compared to previous theories.
3. There are three ways to increase the wage. To increase wage fund by increasing saving, to control number of labourers or to put cut in profit or interest and divert that amount in wage fund. But in reality, to control number of labourers is the only practical and effective remedy, according to this theory.
4. This doctrine provided a solid ground to put forward the demand and supply law of wage.
5. According to this theory, wage depends on two factors. *Viz.*, number of labourers and wage fund. In this way this theory has been represented analytically and systematically.
6. This theory can be represented in the form of equation as under...

$$\text{Wage} = \frac{\text{Wage Fund}}{\text{Supply of labourers}}$$

Suppose, wage fund is Rs. 20,000 lakhs and number of labourers are 200 lakhs.

Therefore,

$$\text{Wages} = \frac{20{,}000}{200} = 100$$

Now, if wage fund remains same, but number of labourers increases to 400 lakhs.

Therefore,

$$\text{Wages} = \frac{20{,}000}{400} = 50$$

Thus, as number of labourers increases, wage decreases, because wage fund does not increase.

(B) *Criticisms* :

1. Practically owner's don't keep such wage funds.
2. If population increase, wage would decrease, that matter is not Practical in today's context.
3. It doesn't look logical that wage fund is constant and non-convertible.
4. According to this theory, wage fund is constant, so if wage increases in one industry, it decreases in other industries. But in reality if wage increases in one industry it is increases in other industries too.
5. This theory can't explain about wage differences.
6. Today in new industries, where capital is less, wages are high. While in old industries where capital is more, wages are low. This matter is contradictory to the heart of the theory.
7. In this theory, it is not explained, how wage fund is determined.
8. Wages depend on productivity or efficiency of the labourers and not on the wage fund or number of labourers. This theory has not been taken into account this matter.
9. This theory cannot explain about the fact that wage increases due to owner's competition to get labourers and lock-out activities.
10. This concept says that demand of the labour is supposed to be constant and wage is decided on the basis of its supply, So it is a partial concept.
11. This concept is mathematical. But it's not practical.
12. Thornet says that owners do not maintain two different funds *viz.*, for their personal use and for the wages of labourers.
13. It's not true that demand of labour is caused only by wage fund.
14. Wage rate also effects demand of labour and supply of labour. But it is not accepted here.
15. There is no novelty. It just narrates established and proved fact.
16. In this theory, only supply of quantitative or physical labour has been considered but qualitative supply of labour has been not taken into account.
17. This doctrine represents non-scientifically and illogical matters.
18. This principle is also unrealistic as it cannot explain the fact, that wage is decided by many factors.

19. It's main hypothesis is combinative, illogical and unrealistic.
20. Here labour is considered to be uniform. But this concept can't explain why there is inequality in wages.
21. Some complications are observed in representation statements and explanation of this theory.

Thus, although there are some defects in this theory, its some vital conclusion are considered important even today. Ricardo, Adam Smith and Malthus made supportive representation, but there is a special importance of systematic representation, which was done by J.S. Mill.

(iv) Residual Claimant Theory

(A) *Representation and Explanation of the Doctrine* :

According to this theory labour has right over whatever residual remains after paying to the factors of production except labour. This residual is paid to the labourer as wage.

First of all, Adam Smith represented this theory. Jevons too expressed his thoughts about it. But Walker tried to give it systematic form.

According to Walker, industrial produce can be divided into four parts : Rent, Wage, Interest and Profit. According to economic concepts, Rent, Interest and Profit divided from the production. Whatever, remains after payment of these three factors, is given to the labourers in the form of wage. Thus, labourers receive what remains in the end.

"The wages of a working man are ultimately coincident with what he produces after the deduction of rent, taxes and interest of capital."

(B) *Characteristics of the doctrine* :

1. In this doctrine efficiency or productivity of labour is taken for consideration.
2. It is accepted that, in the long run, labourer shall get the benefit of increased productivity or increased efficiency. As productivity increases production and income also increases. So, wage increases, because amount of labourer's share also increases.
3. This theory is based on the concept that labourers should get due share from the national income.
4. Its representation and explanation is effective, realistic and proper compared to previous concepts.
5. This theory can explain about various differences and varieties of wages.
6. Theory of marginal productivity get good support, through (by) this theory.
7. This concept is superior to the theory of marginal productivity and theory of living wage. It's a combination of both the concepts.

8. According to Walker, labourers gets what remain after deducting rent, interest and profit from the total production. Jevons says that wage is paid to the labourers after deduction of rent, tax and interest on capital from the production. This can be shown in the equation form as under :

   Wage = Total production – (Rent + Interest + Profit)

(C) *Defects/Limitations of the Theory* :

1. In this theory there is no base for deciding wage. To say that whatever remains in the end, is the part of the wage, is not proper. The way in which interest, rent and profit is determined, in the same way (manner) wage is decided.
2. Supply of labour plays major role in deciding wage. This fact was not considered in this theory.
3. It is not proper to say that labourer shall get their share as wages, from whatever remains the end. Because organiser, has right over the residuals after paying expenses of production and not the labourers.
4. This theory can't explain how Labour Union's activities effect wages.
5. The sum remaining in the end is variable and indefinite. So wage also becomes variable and indefinite.
6. Labourer's wage cannot be decided differently. As value of production factors is being fixed, in the same manner value of labour can be fixed.
7. If production and income increase due to increased productivity of labour, then only labourer is not beneficial but other means of production also get benefit, because labourer gets whatever remains after paying to the other means.

(v) Karl Marx's Theory of Exploitation

(A) *Representation and Explanation* :

According to Karl Marx only labourer is responsible for creation of value, but he does not get its full advantage. He receives only minimum wage. Thus, total residual value, profit of the producer, is received through exploitation of labourer.

According to Marx, in capitalistic economy, owners give less wage to the labourers and exploit them; thus, they earn more profit. They give only minimum living wage to the labourer from their production. Karl Marx says, "residual value to whatever remains in the end Capitalists retain this residual value."

Owners are powerful than labourers. They have more bargaining power. They give less wage to labourers with a view to get more profit through residual value.

(B) *Characteristics* :

1. According to Karl Marx theory, how capitalists increase their profit, in capitalistic system can be explained.
2. Explanation of Karl Marx of scientific socialism can be explained through this theory.
3. This theory can explain about capitalism and its downfall.
4. Karl Marx does not agree that wage increases because of increased demand of labour, due to capital investment.
5. In capitalistic system, efforts are made to decrease labour when its demand increases. For that, capitalistic technology is being adopted. So demand of labour goes down ; as a result of it, supply of labourer increases and wage rate goes down.

(C) *Limitations* :

1. It has been represented that the production cost of a commodity is decided according to labour used for it. But actually cost of a commodity is not decided on the basis of its labour
2. Here it is said that, only minimum living wage is given to the labourers. But actually labour is getting more wage than it. Karl Marx's theory cannot explain about it.
3. According to this doctrine, profit of the owner can be increased by exploitation of the workers (labourers) and giving them low wage. But this belief is also not true, because owner can increase their profit by increasing efficiency and technological improvement.
4. By this doctrine, whatever explanation Marx has given for demand of labour and capitalism; production system is not realistic too. Mostly owners are using labour saving techniques. So supply of labourers exceeds demand of labourers. This matter does not seem true, that as a result wages goes down.
5. This theory put forward only negative side and thinks about only exploitation of labourers.
6. Efficiency of labourers is not taken for consideration in this theory. It cannot explain about effects of labourers' productivity on wages.
7. On the basis of this doctrine Karl Marx predicted about development and downfall of capitalism. Owners earn more profit by exploiting workers *i.e.*, labourers; and giving them low wage. They unanimously revolt against capitalism, when they are being exploiting too much. And this leads to downfall of capitalism. But Karl Marx's this theory is irrelevant in present context because now a days profit is not symbol of exploitation.

REFERENCE

1. Ram Avtar, Lectures on Labour Problems and Social Welfare in India, p. 191.

2

Theories of Wages — 2

"Labour Income can be raised faster and further through growth of national output than through redistribution of national output."

—*R.N. Sinha*

Outline of the Chapter

1. Theory of Marginal Productivity :
   - (i) Meaning and explanation of marginal productivity of labour.
   - (ii) How marginal productivity can be obtained.
   - (iii) Presentation and explanation of the doctrine.
   - (iv) Explanation of equilibrium according to marginal productivity.
   - (v) Different views on doctrine of marginal productivity.
   - (vi) Evaluation of theory.
2. Theory of demand and supply of labour :
   - (i) Presentation and explanation of the theory.
   - (ii) Demand of labour.
   - (iii) Supply of labour
   - (iv) Demand and supply of labour in rural labour market.
   - (v) Evaluation of the theory.
3. Theory of Collective Bargaining of Wage :
   - (i) Challenge to the traditional concept of wage determination.
   - (ii) Wage determination through collective bargaining.
   - (iii) Political management of labour unions.
   - (iv) Financial and political effects on collective bargaining.
   - (v) Collective bargaining and wage paying capacity.
   - (vi) Importance and peculiarities of the theory.
   - (vii) Drawbacks of theory.

Conclusion

1. THEORY OF MARGINAL PRODUCTIVITY

(i) Meaning and explanation of marginal productivity of labour

Labour is a joint contribution of mental or physical work done by labourer, in the return of the wages. Marginal labour means last or ultimate unit of labour. Productivity means rate of net increasing in production. Thus, marginal productivity of labour means net increase in the production, due to protecting one more labourer in production work.

According to Prof. Marshall, wage will be as equal to net production. So it can be said that he too represents theory of marginal productivity of wages. Production increase rate is represented by productivity. Productivity is a measurement of efficiency, it is attached with 2 variable factors. It shows connection between factors and production. It is expressed in the form of net increase rate, and not in the form of total quantity. It is calculated in reference of a unit.

Productivity of labour represents relation between labour and net production increase rate but to measure of labour productivity is a big problem. There are some problems to measure it properly. Work hours can be measured as clearly as capital tools. Yet man-hours are considered as measurement of efficiency. So productivity of man-hour is known as 'labour productivity'. So it can be said that labour productivity means "labour measured, in reference of number, in reference of production, increase."

Now let's look at the factors which effect productivity of labour. It can be said that the factors which affects the number of man-hours and which effects quantity of labour, all these factors effect productivity. Number and quantity of tools, which labourers use for production, also effects production. Factors like, Quantity of raw material, production system, administrative skill, benefit of new system etc. directly effects productivity. Other effecting factors to the productivity are flow of available capital, government's policy of controlling monopoly, encouragement to the competition, volume of business, nature of economic activity etc.

Atmosphere and climates also effect productivity of labour. Standard of labourers' skill, their educational and intellectual level, hygiene, moral, grasping, mobility, inspiration and tendency, all these factors shall decide volume of production during man-hours.

Labour is not the sole instrument of production. So when we talk about production we don't mean it as production done by labourers. We only think, how labourers are responsible in production in context with capital, land, entrepreneur etc. factors.

If we keep other tools of production constant and increase number of labourers in working units, then net increase in production is marginal productivity of labour. In the same way, by increasing labourers the net per labourer increase in production can be called marginal productivity of labour.

(ii) How Marginal Productivity can be obtained

In fact it is very difficult to obtain marginal productivity, many factors affects on it. These factors are closely connected with each other. It is very difficult task to scientifically classify the factors affecting productivity.[1] Yet, various economists and experts have expressed their views at different times regarding determining marginal productivity. Adam Smith[2], Ronald Gibson[3], Rostas[4], Sreenivasan[5] etc. are among them. The factors affecting on labour's productivity are divided into four parts by International Labour Organisation, namely, (1) Common factors; (2) Organisational factors, (3) Technical factors and (4) Human factors.[6]

V.B. Singh[7] says, "It is rather a sociological phenomenon depending upon a number of factors such as increased employment, higher efficiency, increase in industrial investment and above all the adoption of productivity techniques." In fact productivity of labour depends upon following main factors :

1. Quantitative and qualitative number of labourers.
2. Investment, Capital formation and Technology.
3. Managerial system.
4. Working hours.
5. Working conditions.
6. Implementation of factory law.
7. Policy of administrators.
8. Economic and non-economic incentives.
9. Earning of labour.
10. Education and training.

On the basis of all these factors labour productivity is determined and from it wage is fixed. Asian Productivity Council also tried to measure productivity.

According to it, technical, human and organisational factors are prime factors which directly affecting to productivity of labour. This approach can be identified as a "Total factor productivity approach" or can be known as managerial analysis in context with productivity function of 'Macro' units.

Survey of labour productivity was conducted by Japan's Ministry of Laobur between 1952 and 1986. This has been conducted according to sampling method on behalf of International Labour Organisation.

In India analysis pertaining to productivity of labour has been represented by National Productivity Council (NPC) which is an active member of A.P.O.

(iii) Presentation and Explanation of the Doctrine

According to this theory, labour is being given wages, as equal to its marginal productivity, wage of labour should be fixed on the basis of its marginal productivity and labourers should be kept accordingly. By keeping labourers, the average productivity and marginal productivity will be more than wages. But as number of labourer rises average productivity (A.P.) and marginal productivity (M.P.) decreases, and at one stage wages and marginal productivity become equal. (M.P. = W). Now producer does do not keep more labourer. Thus, wages and marginal productivity becomes equal.

This can be shown from following table :

Units of Labourers	Total Production	Average Production	Marginal Production	Price	Average Revenue	Marginal Revenue	Wages
In Units	Units	Units	Units	Rs.	Rs.	Rs.	Rs.
1	6	6.0	6	1.00	6.00	6.00	
2	13	6.5	7	1.00	6.50	7.00	5.00
3	21	7.0	8	1.00	7.00	8.00	5.00
4	28	7.0	7	1.00	7.00	7.00	5.00
5	34	6.8	6	1.00	6.80	6.00	5.00
6	39	6.5	5	1.00	6.50	5.00	5.00
7	43	6.1	4	1.00	6.10	4.00	5.00
8	46	5.8	3	1.00	5.80	3.00	5.00

It can be seen from the table that, when 3 labourers are employed, marginal income, average income, average production and total production are more than wages. But after keeping 4th labourer, average production become constant, and marginal production also decrease. But here wage is less than marginal production. By employing 5th labourer average production decreases and marginal production also decreases. But still wage is less. When 6th labourer is employed, value of marginal production and wages become equal. Now marginal production value will be less than wages if more labourers would be employed, which producer cannot afford. Thus, equilibrium obtained between factor of labour and production, when wage and marginal production value is equal. Now producer cannot employ more labourers for production.

This can be represented in brief as under :

1. Wage is determined on the basis of marginal productivity. Labourer should get wages as equal to his marginal productivity.
2. The producer would employ only that much labourers just when marginal productivity and wage become equal.
3. In the beginning marginal productivity is more than wages, but as number of labourer increases, marginal productivity decreases and at one stage it becomes as equal to wages.
4. When other factors of production are kept constant and number of labourers are increased, then in the beginning, average physical production, marginal physical production, average income and marginal income increase. But then it declines.
5. For the measuring of marginal productivity of labour, factors except labour are kept constant and units of labour are increased.
6. It is assumed that units of labour and units of production have homogeneous.

(iv) Explanation of Equilibrium According to Marginal Productivity

It can be said that situation of equilibrium is achieved when marginal cost and revenue become equal. For this situation it is necessary that marginal productivity of labour and wage given to labour should be equal. Something can be said about other factors also.

The proportion of change in production depends on the prices of the factors of production. Prices of the factors depend upon prices of production. This explanation was presented by Prof. Chamberlin.

Now let's try to understand this through formula and equation.

The interpretation of code words are as following :

MPP = Marginal Physical Production

(big) P = Price of Production

(small) P = Price of factors

a, b... = Factors

A, B... = Produce.

Here we assume that factors of production and production are homogeneous. So there is no difference in their units.

In this example, in context with a, b... n as factors and A, B... N are presented as product. When price of a, b... n becomes equal to A, B... N then the firm achieves equilibrium position.

In other word it can be said that when factor price and product price becomes equal, then position of equilibrium takes place. This happens only, when productivity of factors and price of factors become equal. This phenomenon is presented in the form of equation as under :

$$\frac{\text{MPPa (A)} \times \text{Pa}}{\text{Pa}} = \frac{\text{MPPb (A)} \times \text{Pa}}{\text{Pb}} = \ldots \frac{\text{MPPn (A)} \times \text{Pa}}{\text{Pn}} \quad \ldots. (1)$$

$$\frac{\text{MPPa (B)} \times \text{Pb}}{\text{Pa}} = \frac{\text{MPPb (B)} \times \text{Pb}}{\text{Pb}} = \ldots \frac{\text{MPPn (B)} \times \text{Pa}}{\text{Pn}} \quad \ldots. (2)$$

$$\frac{\text{MPPa (N)} \times \text{Pn}}{\text{Pa}} = \frac{\text{MPPb (N)} \times \text{Pb}}{\text{Pb}} = \ldots \frac{\text{MPPn (N)} \times \text{Pn}}{\text{Pn}} \quad \ldots. (3)$$

It can be said that, when these three N become equal to 1 (one) then condition of equilibrium is proved. Thus, equilibrism situation obtained when factor price and production price become equal. And this equilibrium condition is only fulfilled, when factor price and productivity is same. Now suppose L is labour and A is product then,

$$\frac{\text{MPPL(A)} \times \text{Pa}}{\text{PL}} = 1.$$

In this context, it can be said that equilibrium can be achieved in context with "Labour" as a factor and 'A' as a product. Wages paid to the labour become equal to its marginal productivity. Hence, production cost of labour and wage become equal. Now production of 'A' will change, only if, "Price of 'L' changes, and price of 'L' depends upon price of 'A'."

(v) Different Views on Doctrine on Marginal Productivity

This doctrine is one of the important doctrine among modern theories of wages. Opinions of the learned experts and economists regarding doctrine of marginal productivity can be briefly summarised as under :

1. *P.R.N. Sinha*[8] says labourers also get benefit due to increase in production. Labour income can be raised faster through growth of national output than through redistribution of national output.[9]

   It is very essential to increase production in the country. It has been emphasised to get sure to increase production in reference to independence. Increase in production without affecting factors of production is necessary.[10] Increase in wages, without increasing production shall not be fruitful, because good effects of wage increase will be eliminated due to price hike.

2. *Prof. Marshall* believed that wage is as equal to net production. Theory of Marginal Productivity is not independent theory of wage, but it is a part of General Theory of Value. According to this theory, price of the commodity has approach to become as equal as the cost made after it. Similarly value of labour is also determined.
3. *International Labour Organisation* has observed in its publication "Methods of Labour Productivity Statistics" that organisational factors, technical factors, human factors are affects of production of labour.
4. *Mrs. Jhon Rebinson* Believes that wage is determined on the basis of marginal productivity of labour. So if a labourer is given less wage than his marginal productivity, it can be called exploitation of labour.
5. *Prof. Chamberlin* opined that state of equilibrium is achieved when price of factors production become same.
6. *Asian Productivity Council* believed that wage is a value of labour. It is determined according to marginal productivity of labour. This institution has presented an analysis in context with total factor productivity.
7. *V.B. Singh* says that concept of productivity of labour is basically a social concept. Productivity of labour depends upon rise in employment, more efficiency, rise in industrial investment and acceptance of high productivity technique.

(vi) Evaluation of Theory

(1) *Peculiarities of Marginal Productivity Theory* :

1. This theory is considered to be one of the modern important theories. It has been scientifically represented. It is supreme or superior to previous theories of wages.
2. The theory of marginal productivity of labour emphasises regarding fair wage and work-oriented wage.
3. Wage boards also observe efficiency or productivity of labour while fixing the wage.
4. Producers also prefer to say wages according to marginal productivity. They believe that the minimum wages should be fixed on the basis of work. Labour's real income shall go down, proportion of employment shall decrease, production cost shall go up and inflationary pressures shall increase, if wage is fixed without considering production.

5. *R.G. Lipsey* says that this theory is related with demand of factors of production. It provides counterpart of theory of distribution.
6. *Samualson* opined that this theory, explains about only that how a firm would utilise its factors after getting return of the production.
7. *J.B. Clark* says that demand of labour is caused by its production. It is not being demanded by wage fund.
8. In recent years, it has been accepted that marginal productivity can be increased by increase in wage. Not only that management also can be efficient by it.
9. This theory supported to the collective bargaining.
10. Efforts has been made to eliminate drawbacks of previous theories.

(2) *Drawbacks of the theory* :

1. Practical implementation of this theory is very difficult, because it is very difficult to determine marginal productivity of labour, so wage boards find difficults to use this theory.
2. According to the committee on fair wage, productivity is a combined result of all factors. Even labourers do not have control over some of the factors. So in its words "In connection with the productivity of labour, it has also be remembered that it is the net result of a number of factors on many of which the worker does not exercise any control."
3. It is natural that practical utility of this theory decreases, because scientific methods to measure marginal productivity of labour does not exist.
4. Productivity is being effected by many factors, certain effect of certain factor cannot be known.
5. It has been believed in this theory that factors of labour are homogeneous. This is not true in practice.
6. This theory is based on hypothesis of perfect competition, while in practice perfect competition is not observed.
7. According to Prof. Lipsey in this theory it has been not thought about supply of factors. Only demand of factors have been taken in account.
8. Keynes says that according to this theory employment can be increased by decreasing wage rate. But this opinion does not look true in context with whole economy.
9. According to Crezer, theory of marginal productivity is more deep and objective. Its hypothesis is too rigid and unreal. It is true in only perfect competition.
10. Benham believes that this theory is not true in the point of view of firms.
11. According to Samualson, this theory does not give explanation of price determination of production. It only explains that how

and which proportion a firm invest its factors, if the price of factors is given.

12. This theory can be explained only in the condition of diminishing returns. It cannot be explained in constant or increasing return.
13. It is said in theory that wage is determined according to marginal productivity. But actually effects of wage also directly affected to the productivity of labourer.
14. This doctrine explains about long-term wage determination. But it cannot explain about short-term.
15. As it is difficult to determine margin of labourer, it is tough to know marginal productivity.
16. This theory is based on "Marginal Analysis". There are many drawbacks to the analysis, which is applicable to this theory also.
17. It is not explained in theory, how price like effects in wage.

Thus, although there are some drawbacks in this theory, its importance does not decrease. It is very important modern theory. It has practical as well as theoretical importance.

2. THEORY OF DEMAND AND SUPPLY OF LABOUR

(i) Presentation and Explanation of Theory

The price of labour is decided by its supply and demand like other commodities. The general theory of price-determination, means theory of demand and supply. The theory of wage is not a separate theory, but it is a internal part of general price determination.

This theory says that, wage is the price of labour, so wage is decided according to demand and supply of labour. Wage decreases, if demand of labour remains constant, and supply increases. And if supply decreases, the wage increases. Similarly if supply of labour remains constant, and its demand increases, then wage increases and *vice versa.*

The demand of labour is different from demand of commodity. Owner's demand of labour depends upon availability of sum of investment. The Capital investment depends on marginal productivity of capital. Capital supply depends on availability of savings and savings depends on rate of interest.

Demand of labour and wage rate is effected by excess by employee. The demand of labour decreases if excess investment is being done in labour saving machines. So workers become willing to work at lower wage due to competition. The supply of labour depends upon proportion of labour force, population growth rate, proportion of wage etc. Thus, demand and supply of labour is different from demand and supply of other commodities.

(ii) Demand of Labour

Any individual firm asks for labour according to its factor combination. The labour depends upon, how long capital and labour can act as each other's substitute. It also depends on productivity growth rate. The demand of labour is also dependent on price of labour and price of product which means on the marginal cost, and on marginal income.

In other words, marginal production value plays vital role in deciding demand of labour. Marginal production value can be achieved by multiplying marginal physical product (MPP), by the market price of product.

Means MPV = MPP × p

The producer shall try to co-ordinate all factors in such a way that marginal production value of each factor shall be equal to the price of that factor (PF) means MPV = PF.

Suppose A, B, C are three factors, than he shall co-ordinate them in such a manner and proportion that marginal production value of all these shall be equal to their value in equation, it can be presented like this :

$$\frac{MPVA}{PA} = \frac{MPVB}{PB} = \frac{MPVC}{PC}$$

As law of diminishing return prevails in production field, the marginal production value shall decrease if the factor units are more. And it shall increase, if factor units are less. Thus, we observe that producer shall project all factors, including labour in such a manner that marginal production value of all factors shall be same. But the changes according to alternatives shall be made, when marginal production value of two factors shall not be same. But when marginal production value of both factors are same, then there is no need for alternation, so proportion of factors is kept constant.

Suppose marginal production value of labour is 160 and wage is 80 and marginal production value of capital is 30, and its price is 15.

$$\text{Means} \quad \frac{MPVL}{PL} = \frac{MPVC}{PC}$$

$$= \frac{160}{80} = \frac{30}{15}$$

$$= \frac{16}{8} = \frac{30}{15} = 2$$

Here production of factors shall not be changed because marginal productive value of both factors is same.

Now, suppose, capital cost becomes double :

$$\frac{16}{8} = \frac{30}{30}$$

Here producer shall be benefited by reducing capital units and increasing labour units. Marginal production value of labour shall decrease by increasing its unit. And marginal productivity value of capital shall increase by decreasing its unit. So it shall be like this :

$$\frac{12}{8} = \frac{45}{30} = \frac{3}{2}$$

Now producer shall not change the proportion of capital and labour, because marginal production value of both has become equal.

Thus, demand of labour shall be made in such a way that marginal production value of labour and wage given to it, becomes equal.

Besides this, demand of labour depends on process of industry and form of the product. There are widespread difference in industrial process. There are also widespread differences in capital factor, raw material and other material for production.

Labour cost plays vital role in deciding, demand of labour. The owners have tendency to increase capital factor, if cost of labour is more.

Time element is one of the prime factors deciding demand of labour. It may be possible that, demand of labour is not constant, but it is seasonal.

Besides this, the process changes and technological changes also effect demand of labour. In short, following factors are main factors effecting demand of labour :

1. Proportion of capital investment.
2. Marginal productive value of labour.
3. Alternative proportion of capital factor.
4. Production process.
5. Form of product.
6. Proportion of labour cost.
7. Time element.
8. Cyclical changes.
9. Technological changes.
10. Production process and production structure.

The wage is effected by demand of labour and changes in it.

(iii) Supply of Labour

Supply of labour plays vital role in deciding wages. Real wage and money wage is effected by proportion of unemployment, in under-developed nations. According to Arthur Lewis, Rural workmen shall get less wages, unless and until they are absorbed in cities/industries.

As a result of this, there shall be two sections : Modern urban section and agriculture-oriented rural section.

Population growth is also a prime factor which effects labour supply.

The nation where population growth rate is high, there shall be more supply of unskilled workers. So they shall be ready to work at low wage.

(1) Backward Bending Labour-Supply Curve. In underdeveloped nations, there is shortage of literature, or research work, regarding backward sloping labour supply line.[11] It is necessary to understand two approaches to understand this analysis theoretically.

1. Such antitrend is observed due to change in income and Alternative effects.
2. Here concept of income effects is important.

According to Josef Hardar the customer wishes to earn a certain income. And with the change in wage rate, he makes adjustment to maintain desired income level.[12]

Everett Hagen has studied backward sloping labour supply curve in context with American and South Asian nations. He narrated in his studies that workers living nearby return to their home after working some time in mine or they have gone outside the town. They return to home when their wage is increased at the end of year, to encourage the function of workers. The labourers cannot obtain more wage, than a certain wage.[13] Thus supply of labour is not effected by rise in money wage.

Traditional Economic Concept explains intelligent behaviour of customer in reference to utility analysis. He decides to achieve a certain sum to achieve target of certain utility. And he dedicates his labour for same.

But after getting that sum, he does not prefer to more work to get more income. So this labour supply line is backward sloping. It shows that in initial phase labourer prefer more work and less leisure. While in later phase he prefers less work and more leisure. So supply of labour does not increase even though wage increases.

(2) Factors Effecting Labour Supply. The labourer can be defined on the basis of his position in labour force in the labour market, and type of the work which he performs to get wage. Labour is a different factor than other factors. A person is attached in the production process by his labour. There is difference between workers on the basis of ownership and other factor of production. Labour and labourers are undividable. Labour cannot be accumulated, while other means are separate from owners. And they can be stored.

Volume/size of the population is most important factor, effecting supply of the labour. The more supply of labour is available, where there is more population in nation. Similarly age group is also vital factor effecting labour supply. More labour supply can be obtained if proportion of labour offering class, means people between age of 15 years to 45 years are more in numbers.

The proportion of participation in labour force lose of the time due to let go the leisure ultimately. He reaches at a point, where rise in one matter, can be done only at the cost of other. This matter can be said less desirable.

According to Indian traditions head of the family spends more time in earning, women in household duties and children spend time in education.

Head of family shall project women and children in labour works, till necessary income to run the family is not achieved. But now, with the rise in wages he gets some income by less labour. So he shall withdraw women and children from labour work. Now he shall try to buy leisure and would prefer combination of less work and more comfort.

Thus, with rise in the wages, the head of family will withdraw women, children and adults from labour. But if his wage decreases then he shall not work for more hours. But shall force other family members to work.

(3) Supply of Labour in Long Duration. The classical economists said that there shall be early marriage due to increase in the wage. Hence, families shall be large and wage shall be low due to increase in the labour supply. But modern economist do not accept this concept. They say that with the rise in the wage, literacy shall increase, living standard shall go high, workers shall prefer small family. So population will decrease.

The work of workers depends on comparative wage rate, if other conditions are equal. If we assume, of labour supply, with reference to one firm, and accept the theory of maximisation, then we can say that workmen shall prefer to give their labour to high paying firm to low paying firm. The workers working in low paying firm, will be attracted towards high paying firms. Thus, propotion of workers will be towards high wages.

Worker shall try to get maximum economic gain, by comparing utility and non-utility.

Labourers shall be willing to work at low wages due to more labour supply, migration, population growth and slack condition.

(4) Reconsideration of Labour Supply. It seems essential to reconsider regarding traditional theory of labour supply. People are interested in the wages, coming by the sale of labour and they desire to get it more. People wish to have more income. But for that they have to depend on many factors. They have to make selection of the profession, considering factors like, method and form of the duty, work, behaviour of the supervisor or employee, working condition, job satisfaction etc., and tries to gain income accordingly.

From all these matters, it can be said that labour supply is not dependent only on wages, or labourer has to make not only selection between leisure and labour but he has to think so many factors before giving their labour.

It is essential to reconsider about labour supply. Because concept of backward sloping labour supply line and selection between leisure and labour has become irrelevant.

(iv) Demand and Supply of Labour in Rural Labour Market

A study for wage determination and rural labour market was held in context to Uttar Pradesh, was held by Papola, T.S. and V.N. Misra.[14] In some studies, it was found that, labour market is competitive and wage is decided according to law of Demand and Supply. But in some studies, it was found that it is not determined in this manner due to structural rigidity. The wage rate is not effected by demand and supply of labour. There accur many changes in demand and supply of labour. The labour market is different from other market, on the basis of quality due to rigidity of labour market. There is no effect of wage rate on rural labour supply. This study says that unemployment of agriculture workers are so high, that the condition of inter relation between wages and demand and supply of rural labour market get confused. During A certain period of year, large number of supply seems to be surplus. It increases the labour force and converts labour supply into labour, at any wage rate.[15] The quantity of such labour force is different according to area. In rural area family and society, prefer to engage the worker at home. So they do not prefer to move out.[16]

It has been observed that sufficient use of workers is not being done in agriculture. Only half of the possible labour force is being utilised.[17]

In rural labour market contribution of female workers seems to be very less. This labour force becomes available, only if need arises. But in some sectors, where women can do better agriculture work, at that place participation of women is more. In developed countries, it has been observed that participation of women in whole labour force is positive with reference to wage rate but it is negative with reference to total family income.[18]

Rule of limited need is applied where farming is being done for sustenance. Because here production cannot be increased and more labour is not used from available sources.[19]

It becomes essential to increase women labour supply, because with the rise in the cost the living expense increases, and more earning becomes necessary. Thus, there is negative relationship between female labour supply and wage rate, because contribution of women labour supply decreases with increase in wage.

There is negative relationship between women labour and income level. This can be shown by backward sloping women labour supply line. It can be explained by 'U' shape. It indicate that in initial phase of development, rate of contribution goes down. But it goes up in later phase. Means, in starting period, women have to compete with men, for job. But due to increase in the wage, their participation becomes less. But women labour contribution has to be increased, when income is less than living wage, which is presented by 'U' shape. The contribution of women will be withdrawn as soon as income reaches at the living wage level. This condition will come when production increases and wage of male worker shall go high. Thus, income level decides the contribution of female labour.

(v) Evaluation of Theory

1. This is very important theory in which, wage determination explained systematically. Like other prices, the wage is also decided according to demand and supply.
2. This theory is well balanced because equal importance has been given to demand and supply of labour.
3. Here it is said that theory of wage is basically a part of theory of value.
4. Productivity of labour is also considered in this doctrine, because the demand of labour is done according to marginal productivity of labour.
5. Function of labour market and prices of wage determination can be easily explained by this theory.

   Although this is very important theory, there are some limitations in it.

Limitations of the Theory

1. Wage determination can not be explained by general law of demand and supply. Because demand and supply of labour is different from that of other commodity.
2. There are many rigidity in labour market. So factor of demand and supply do not effect wages.

3. There are two types of labour market. Both of them have different properties.
4. It is difficult to predict or measure, demand and supply of labour.
5. A general theory can not be given regarding effect of demand and supply of labour on wages. Because it is variable according to different notations and different approaches.

   In spite of many limitations, the theory of demand and supply of labour is very important, because it can explain wage-determination process scientifically.

3. THEORY OF COLLECTIVE BARGAINING OF WAGE

(i) Challenge to the Traditional Concept of Wage Determination

Labour union activities have fairly developed in modern time, after industrial revolution. With the development of labour unions, the concept of collective bargaining has been implemented. The wage is decided by collective bargaining. The government has made laws for labour welfare, and taken steps in this regard. Agreements, social and economic factors, government's laws, judgements of court, etc. factors play major role in fixing wages and its implementation. So one challenge has arisen against traditional concept of wage determination. Today traditional concept of wages has become less effective due to factors effecting wage.

Today inter-process of wage determination is of the different form in which factors except, demand and supply or marginal productivity effect the wages. The factor except living wage, life sustenance and wage fund, plays major role in determining wage. Due to collective bargaining, the industries have been divided in two sections, *viz.*, high wage level industries and low wage level industries.

Today real wage is also considered besides monetary wage. So wage is being increased to maintain real wages, with the increase in the prices. Employer, labour unions, and effects of labour unions on collective bargaining, have clear effect on wage structure. There is difference in wage fixation process of private sectors and public sectors. The wage is effected by anti-inflationary policy of Government and political steps. This matter has been not presented in the traditional concept of wage. So a challenge is raised against it. So, it is essential to present the concept with different angle. The concept of collective bargaining is such special concept.

This theory explains how wage is decided according to strength of the unions. This theory explains, how wage is fixed and changed due to collective bargaining between employers and workers.

(ii) Wage Determination Through Collective Bargaining

There are two sides in fixing wages. Employers and workers. The employers do not wish to give more wage, because it increases their production cost. It also effects their profit. On the other side the workers try to get maximum wages with context to continuous rise in the living expense, because wage is the only source of their income. The labourers shall be able to get higher wages, they are united and their union is strong. But they shall get less wages, if they are not united and the union is not strong. Because here the collective bargaining of employers are stronger than workers.

There are two trends in the industries on the basis of collective bargaining :

(a) High pay giving industries.

(b) Low pay giving industries.

The collective bargaining has failed in majority nations to solve the problems of low wages. The wages remain low due to poor collective bargaining. So legal procedures become necessary. In this conditions, government makes minimum wage rules and provides economic protection to the workers. These efforts are made by collective bargaining, or government to solve the problem of low wage.

The labour unions try to make maximum wage bill. And they constantly try to obtain maximum allowances and benefits for their members. But the collective bargaining become limited because financial capacity and conditions play vital role in deciding wages. The commodity market decides financial capacity of a firm. The labour union use pressure methods to get more wages than what employer is willing to give voluntarily. Unions succeed to get more wages, if they have monopoly over labour power.

(iii) Political Management of Labour Unions

"The wage is decided according to collective bargaining." That interpretation has been challenged. Some experts believe that labour unions cause certain 'Political' effects whose independent effect, effects the wage determination. These political effects, do not care about market factors and it is more effective than the effect of collective bargaining.

The workers compare their wage, with the wages of other company's workers. And presume how much wages they should get. They also compare their increment with the increments given by employers of other companies. By this comparison, they make demand of wage increase through their leaders of the union. These leaders shall assess that whether they shall be successful to get rise in the wage compared to other unions. They study the strategy adopted by successful unions. And after that negotiations are made with the employers. They either succeed or fail to get increase in wage. This can be said as 'Political' pressure on wage. But it cannot be told 'Economic Pressure' on wage policy, because workers and union leaders, proceed only after studying wage increase obtained by workers and unions of other companies. The success of these 'Political Factor' depends on financial capacity of firm or industry.

(iv) Financial and Political Effects on Collective Bargaining

The success of collective bargaining depends on both economic factors and political effects, if demand of wage increase is made under political influence. But if financial condition shows that it is not in the interest of workers and employer to increase the wage, then political effects become less effective due to economic influence.

Thus, political and economic, both factors effect the collective bargaining. And sometimes economic factor is more powerful than the political factor.

(v) Collective Bargaining and Wage Paying Capacity

The success of collective bargaining depends on so many economic factors. The employers capacity to pay wage is one of the important economic factor. But how can be wage capacity decided? The fair wage committee has said that it is improper to consider a single unit, or to consider wage capacity of all industries of nation, while deciding wage capacity of industry. But actually the wage capacity of a certain industry in certain area must be considered, and wage capacity of all units of one area should be decided in the equal manner.

Indian Supreme Court has given guidelines to test the wage capacity in a case regarding Express Newspaper.

These guidelines are as under :

1. Total productivity of industry (Present/Future)
2. Selling price of product.
3. Cost of raw material
4. The wage rate, which is agreeable to majority of employers.
5. Rate of competent firm.
6. Professional profit/loss.
7. Proportion of unemployment.

It is very essential to define wage when we talk about the wage capacity.

According to wage law of 1936, wage means which is presented in monetary form (pay, allowances or other) or what is reflected as condition of job or as a responsibility of employer. Following matters are included in it :

1. Payable according to contracts between two sides or according to court order.
2. Remuneration for the additional work, done by employer or allowance for the work done during holidays.
3. Remuneration payable as the compensation of other holidays, as per job contracts.
4. Compensation payable after finishing job, as per contract, law or rule.
5. Compensation payable during the job.

(vi) Importance and Peculiarities of the Theory

The theory of collective bargaining is very important in the theory of wage fixation, its importance or peculiarities can be described in brief as following :

1. This theory is more effective and realistic than other.
2. In this theory, it is not needed to take base of unrealistic hypothesis.
3. Effective and real explanation of wage determination process can be given by this theory.
4. It is believed that there shall be unemployment if wage is given more than marginal productivity. But this theory says that the marginal productivity can be increased by higher wage. The firm can cut other expenses to compensate with additional wage expenses. And maximum rise in production can be achieved by the best administration.
5. The fear of unemployment, due to rise in wage and hence decrease in labour supply is irrelevant.
6. This theory is practically observed in market. More employment can be given at higher wage in monopolised competitive market and higher wages can be achieved without creating unemployment if unions are strong.
7. The collective bargaining of workers becomes poor if monopsony of buyer established in the market. So they can not get high wage. In practical field, the workers of the unorganised sectors, get low wages due to their poor bargaining.
8. According to this theory there is no decrease in the investment even if income of the entrepreneur decreases, due to increase in the wage of the workers. Because there is a specific living standard for the consumption for the rich people in which no change takes place. So there is no decrease in their expenses, even if wage increases.
9. In traditional concept of wages, it was believed that cost of

production is decided by labour expense. But now it is accepted that labour expense is a part of total expense. So increase in wage will not much effect on cost of production.

10. The theory of marginal productivity is unrealistic because it says that wage shall be equal to marginal productivity. While the wage achieved by collective bargaining depends on the relative solidity of workers and employers. It shall be possible to get wage increase if unions are strong and there shall not be success if unions are weak.
11. It cannot be said that how much wage shall increase, by collective bargaining. But it shall be fixed somewhere between maximum and minimum of wage rate, according to collective bargaining of employers and workers.
12. This doctrine says that, wage rate is decided free from market factors.
13. Collective bargaining can play vital role in deciding wages. If the employers and workers are flexible, they are ready for negotiations and all facts and figures are available.
14. Workers can get high wage by bargaining if demand of the product is extraordinary, machines cannot be alternative of labour, unions have hold over labour supply, profitability of industry is high, and unions have social support.

All these matters show, efficiency of thus theory and show that it is more practical and effective than other theories. But it also has some limitations.

(vii) Drawbacks of Theory

The main drawbacks of theory is as under :

1. Demand and supply of labour or market factors are not considered in it, while market factors have certain effect on wage-rate.
2. This theory neglects the marginal productivity. And if this theory is accepted then, due to strength of the unions, the workers shall get so high wage, that it shall cross the level of marginal productivity.
3. This is a one-sided theory, because it does not consider wage capacity of industry.
4. The labourers of underdeveloped nations are not united. So their collective bargaining is poor. So they cannot get more wage.
5. Wage is not fixed according to this theory, in the nations where unemployment is more, and profitability of industries is low.
6. John Parrow says that more wages shall lead towards adopting mechanisation.
7. According to John Dui the labour unions can change real income

of workers if exploitation being done. But most probably union activities have very less impaction on total real income of the labour mass.

8. Labour unions are able to obtain higher wages, but creates lot of problems behind it.
9. This theory cannot explain clearly the process of wage determination.
10. Due to politicisation of labour unions, they are not in a position to perform well.

Conclusion

Here we can get idea that the concept of wage is very complex. Many economic and non-economic factors affected on the process of wage-determination. Many economists have tried to throw light on it. Theories of marginal productivity, demand and supply of labour and collective bargaining are the main theories of wages in economics.

REFERENCES

1. Tiwari, R.T. and K.N. Trivedi, "Determinants of Labour's Productivity", *The Indian Journal of Labour Economics*, Vol. XVII, No. 3-4, 1974-75.
2. Adam Smith, *The Wealth of Nation*, p. 7.
3. Ronald Gibson, *Labour Productivity : Cotton Textile Wages in the United States and Great Britain*, 1948, p. 13.
4. Rostas, L., "Output Ahead", *The Times*, November 1946, p.10.
5. Sreenivasan, R., *Productivity and Social Environment*, Bombay, 1964, pp. 19-20.
6. ILO, *Methods of Labour Productivity Statistics*, Geneva, 1951.
7. Singh, V.B. (ed.), *Labour Research in India*, Bombay, 1970, p. 106.
8. Sinha, P.R.N., *Wage Determination*, Asia Publishing House, New Delhi, p. 126.
9. Lloyd & Renolds, *Labour Economics and Labour Relation*, p. 474.
10. Government of India, Planning Commission, *Third Five Year Plan*, p. 262.
11. Ellot Berg, "Backward sloping Labour Supply Function in Dual Economies : The African Case", *Quarterly Journal of Economics*, Vol. 75, August 1961, pp. 468-492.
12. Josef Hardar, *Elementary Theory of Economic Behaviour*, California Addison-Wesley Publishing Co., 1960, pp. 255-256.
13. Everett Hagen, *The Economics of Development*, Home Wood, Illinois : Richard D. Irwin, 1968, pp. 67-68.
14. Papola, T.S. and V.N. Misra, "Labour Supply and Wage Determination in Rural-Uttar Pradesh" June, 1979, Giri Institute, Lucknow.
15. Ladejinsky, W., "The Green Revolution in Punjab : A Field Trip", *Economic and Political Weekly*, Vol. IV, No. 25, June 28, 1969.
16. Papola, T.S., "The Indian Labour Market", *Economic and Political Weekly*, Vol. 111, No. 30, 1968.
17. Sinha, R.C., "Agricultural Development and Rural Employment", in studies on Development of U.P., *Giri Institute of Development Studies*, Lucknow, 1979.
18. Standing, Guy, *Labour Force Participation and Development*, International Labour Office, Geneva, 1978, p. 75.
19. *Ibid.*, p. 61.

3

Concepts of Wages

"It was a wage sufficient to ensure workmen, shelter, clothing, frugal comfort, provision for evil days etc. as well as regard for the special skill of an artisan if he is one."

—*Fair Wage Committee*

Outline of the chapter

1. Share of wages in national Income
   - (i) Opinions of various experts
   - (ii) Factors effecting wage share in national income.
2. Various concepts of wages
   - (1) Fair Wage
     - (i) Meaning
     - (ii) How fair wage is decided
     - (iii) Opinion of Fair Wage Committee
     - (iv) Importance of concept
   - (2) Living wage
     - (i) Meaning and Definition
     - (ii) Determination Method
     - (iii) Importance
     - (iv) Limitations
   - (3) Minimum Wage
     - (i) Definition and Meaning
     - (ii) Determination Method
     - (iii) Implementation in India
     - (iv) Importance
     - (v) Limitations

(4) Monetary wages and real wages
   (i) Meaning
   (ii) Importance
   (iii) In India

1. SHARE OF WAGES IN NATIONAL INCOME

The National income is total of the products and services at current price level. National income is measured, either according to cost of production, or according to sources of income. There are two approaches to calculate the national income. It is achieved, either by the total of the income of all factors of production or it can be obtained by total expense in the economy. Thus, national income can be known by production cost of service and commodities' total expense and total receipt of all factors.

Wages have major role in national income. The distribution pattern of income can be known only by the share of wages in national income. Less share of wages and more share of profit and interest in national income shows unequal distribution of income. That means workers do not get due wage for their work. While the employees snatch major share from cost of production. So the wages must be increased for equal distribution. The wage share in national income is very important. According to concept of marginal productivity, worker gets wage according to his marginal productivity. So, if share of wage is more in national income it means that the workers have major share in total production. In other words workers consume their wages for consumable goods and services. Thus, share of wages in national income is vital on the basis of total income, total expense and total production.

Wage means compensation of work done by worker. The work can be either physical work or mental work. In this context labourers have great contribution in total production. So their wage has important place in national income. From this discussion it is certain that wage share in national income plays major role by aspect of production and aspect of distribution.

(i) Opinions of Various Experts

National income is an important section of macroeconomics. Various experts have given their opinions regarding it. They have also expressed their views, on wage share in national income. Let us see some of the opinions.

(1) *Prof. Adam Smith.* Prof. Adam Smith emphasised on division of labour to increase the national income. According to him the division of labour is the master key for increase in production. He accepted

importance of labour share in national income in total production and national income. According to his opinion rise in the income of worker shall boost up the efficiency and by it demand of commodity shall increase, market shall develop and capital formation shall be speedy.

(2) *Ricardo.* According to Ricardo, there have been changes in the remuneration given to the factors of production in the form of rent, wage or profit from the national income. Availability of wage, profit or rent available from national income depends on certain factors. These factors include fertility of land, investment, proportion of population, efficiency of workers etc.

(3) *Keynes.* Keynes has opposed wage cut policies of classical economists. According to him that belief is not true in the long run that more people can be given employment by wage cut. He told that due to wage cut effective demand shall decrease and due to it, investment shall decrease and unemployment shall increase.

(4) *Prof. Machlup.* He made a specific observation of labourshare in national income. According to him share of labour in national income depends on "Substitute elasticity" between different factors of production. If labour is cheaper than capital then more labour and less capital shall be consumed. So share of wage in national income would be increased. But if capital is cheaper than labour then more capital shall be used and due to that wage share in national income would be decreased.

It depends on production method whether labour and capital can be substitute of each other. They can be substitute of each other only if substitute elasticity is positive. But less units of capital and more unit of labour or less units of capital and more units of labour cannot be used if substitute elasticity is negative. And as a result of it in that condition wage share in national income does not change. Thus, elasticity of substitute can be called negative if use of labour cannot be changed even if cost of labour changes and substitute elasticity can be said positive if consumption of labour increases as its cost decreases.

In this situation use of labour shall increase. Hence, wage share in total national income shall increase.

(5) *Kalecki and Kaldor.* These two experts expressed their views regarding wage share in national income in context to monopoly. According to them the monopolist shall get more share from the production if monopoly power increases. So, wage share in national income decreases. But the share of employer shall decrease and share of the worker shall increase if monopoly power decreases. So wage share in national income shall increase. The wage share in national income depends on cost of raw material in the situation when monopoly power

remains constant. Wage share increases if cost of raw material decreases and wage share decreases if cost of raw material increases. Thus, according to opinion of these experts the wage share in national income depends on "Monopoly power".

(ii) Factors Effecting Wage Share in National Income

The wage share in national income depends on certain factors which are known as factors effecting wage share in national income. The main factors among that can be discussed as under :

(1) Nature of the market. The wage share in national product depends on competition or on the nature of market. The wage share shall be less in monopoly market or oligopoly market. The wage share in national income shall be more if competitive factors are more or the market is competitive.

(2) Job opportunities and proportion of labour force. These labourers shall receive less wage if there is more labour force compared to job opportunities. Because there shall be competition among workers for job, so, they shall be willing to work at lower rate. So, labour share shall be less in national income. Contrary to that workers shall easily get job at higher wage and wage share in national income will be more if labour force is less compared to job opportunities.

(3) Collective bargaining. The wage share in national income depends on collective bargaining. The wage share in national income shall be more if labour unions can play decisive role in wage determination and get success in getting rise in wages. But contrary to that wage share in national income would be less if employers can play effective role in wage fixation. And a result of that workers get less wage.

(4) Flexibility. The labour share in national income shall be variable if the trend of flexibility is more in economy. But the wage share remains constant if economy is rigid. Today economy seems to be flexible, so wage share also remains changing.

(5) Category of economic development. In underdeveloped economy proportion of wage share in national income is more because of importance of labour. While in developed economy proportion of capital is more than that of labour. So, wage share in national income is comparatively less due to mechanisation and adoption of modern labour saving.

(6) Economic system. The wage share in any nation, depends on economic system being adopted. In socialistic economic system the wage share in national income is high because in that system high importance given to the workers and so government arranges for their due wage and other benefits. But in capitalist economic system wage share in national income shall be less because in that system labourers are given less share from national income, due to unequal distribution of income.

(7) Production method. The wage share in national income would be more in national income if labour-oriented production system is widely accepted. But the wage share in national income would be less if capitalistic mechanised production system is adopted. Similarly in agricultural nations wage share will be more, while in industrialist countries wage share shall be less.

(8) Population of workers. The wage share in national income shall be more if there are more workers in population. But the wage share would be less if there are less workers in total population.

(9) Category of workers. The wage share in national income would be more if there are more skilled workers in labour force. But the wage share shall be less if there are more semi-skilled or unskilled workers in total labour force.

(10) Nature of the product. In national income the wage share shall be less if factors other then raw material and labour are more important in production process. But the wage share in national income shall be more if the labour is more important compared to other factors.

(11) Wage level. The wage share in rational income shall be more if there are high wages in whole nation. But wage share would be less if there are low wages in whole nation.

(12) Substitution of labour and capital. The share of wage in national income will be major if substitution of labour and capital is not positive. Because in this condition less capital can be used as option of the labour if the cost of labour increases. It means less substitution and higher share of wage in national income.

(13) Modernization and technological development. The wage share in national income would be less if the nation is modernised and technologically developed. But the wage share would be more if production framework is primitive and technological development is less.

(14) Labour and wage policy. The wage share in national income shall be more if government would be implementing various plans and programmes for labour welfare. And if it making efforts for due wages for the labourers by minimum wage laws and other labour laws. But the wage share shall be less if the government is not interested in workers, and no welfare steps are being taken.

(15) Changes in price level. The proportion of wage in national income would be less if price level is continuously rising and compared to it the rise in wage is less but the wage share shall be more if the rise in wage is more than that of rise in price.

Thus wage share in national income is decided and varies by many factors. Such as demand and supply of labour, economic-system, policy of government, production structure, production method etc.

2. VARIOUS CONCEPTS ON WAGES

(1) Fair Wage

(i) Meaning. Fair wage is one of the important concept among concepts on wages. The fair wages means wage decided by competent authority for the workers working in the same manner and those who have same skill, same problems and same difficulties. According to minimum-wage determination authority of International Labour Organisation the fair wage means the same wage rate for the workers working in the same profession.

Due attention must be given at the initial stage on the workers working in the similar industry or trade. The nations where no proper measurement is available in such nations normal level wage rate is prevailing. According to Marshall if the prevailing wage rate is equal then in such conditions fair wage means wage which is equal to the wages of other profession in which there is equal hardship and in which equal natural efficiency and expensive training is necessary. Prof. Pigu has explained wages in two aspects. *viz.* in narrow concept and in broad concept. According to narrow concept fair wage means if the same wage rate of workers working in the same profession it can be said fair wage. According to broad concept if the wage is similar in all over nation for the same work, and it is common in all trade then it can be said as fair wage.

(ii) How fair wage can be decided. Two concepts are taken in account for deciding fair wage. (1) Living wage and (2) Minimum wage.

Justice Higgins who was attached with the Harvest case of Australian Commonwealth Court has given the most suitable definition of living wage. According to him the wage which can satisfy due need of common worker living in cultural society is called fair wage. According to South Australian law 1932 subsistence living wage means total of fair and proper needs of an average worker who is working at a place or the place where work is going to take place.

The USA Inquiry Committee has explained living wage level by dividing them in 4 parts. (1) Poverty cadre, (2) Minimum subsistences level, (3) Subsistence living plus wage cadre, (4) Comfort wage cadre.

The minimum wage has represented fourth cadre and said that it is considered while deciding fair wage. According to opinion of paper published by minimum wage section of ILO the estimates regarding minimum wage was presented in three sections.

(1) Necessary sum for only sustenance/subsistences.

(2) Sum necessary for Hygine and facilities.

(3) Sum which can satisfy the needs for comfort.

Following points should be considered while deciding fair wage practically :

(1) Productivity, skill and training of labour.

(2) Current wage rate, prevailing in the same profession or places which are nearby.

(3) Proportion of national income.

(4) Role of industry in national income.

(5) Family needs of workers.

(6) Living standard

(7) Future conditions.

According to S.B. Nigam three considerations are included in fair wage :

(1) Workers of same cadre working in same profession should get equal wages.

(2) There should be uniform wage in all professions in one area. And there should be guarantee of equal wage for equal skill.

(3) Different wages should be given according to various training and type of the training.

(iii) Opinion of Fair Wage Committee. The Fair Wage Committee appointed by Government of India submitted its report in 1949.[1] In this report matters on fair wage was broadly discussed. This committee gave definition of fair wage and has given explanation to determine fair wage. According to the recommendation of the committee two concepts should be considered while deciding fair wage :

(1) Concept of minimum wage

(2) Concept of living standard.

The living wage does not consist only food, clothing or shelter. But it also includes all the needs of simple life according to present standard. It has been told by quoting Justice Higgins that, "It was a wage sufficient to ensure workmen food, shelter, clothings, frugal comfort provision for evil days etc. as well as regard for the special skill of an artisan if he is one."

According to the Queensland Industrial and Arbritation Act, a male labourer should be given wage which is enough to maintain his health, energy and compatibility and he can easily look after his wife and family of three children. While fixing this wage the earning of his wife and children must not be considered.

According to the opinion of committee the minimum limit of fair wage should be equal to the minimum wage and maximum limit must be equal to maximum paying capacity of industry. It does not depend only on present economic condition of industry or firm, but also depends on future development.

The committee has suggested to consider about following factors while deciding fair wage between two limits :

(1) Productivity of workers.
(2) The wage rates in professions which are same or nearly same and which are in one area or in the area nearby.
(3) The proportion and distribution of national income.
(4) Position or importance of industry in national economy.

Thus, fair wage committee has suggested to consider about productivity of labour relation of other industries with wages national income and distribution etc. factors.

(iv) Importance of concept. The concept of fair wages is an ideal concept among the concepts regarding giving wages to workers. The fair wage should not be less than the minimum wage. But, it should proceed towards need based wages gradually. It should be enough to satisfactory the family needs of worker.

The needs of workers can be satisfied by fair wage. It can also increase productivity and efficiency of workers and it also maintains industrial peace because workers would not call for strike. The fair wage satisfies most of the financial expectation of workers. The owners also agree for that because they also get reward of the fair wage in the form of increase in production.

(2) Living Wage

(i) Meaning and Definition. Living wage means wage that by which workers can easily look after their family and they are able to live peacefully and comfortably.

According to opinion of Higgins the living wage is the wage by which an average worker can live as a member of cultural society.

The wage should not be only sufficient to satisfy his needs for food, clothing and shelter, but the wage should be such so that he can easily live according to present living standard. He further says that living wage must assure for food, shelter, clothing and provision for evil days. It should be also according to his skill.

(ii) Determination method. According to Queensland Industrial and Arbitration Act the living wage means by which worker can maintain his family consisting of a wife and three children maintaining his own health energy and his stamina for competition. The income of wife and children must not be counted while fixing wage. A survey was held in USA in 1919 regarding Budget Commissionary of Bureau of Labour Statistics analyzed budget in three sections. The poverty line, minimum standard for sustenance and minimum level for hygine and ease. He choose 3rd standard for living wage.

The United Provinces Labour Inquiry Committee has decided living wage in four parts :

(1) poverty level, (2) minimum sustainance level, (3) sustenance plus level, (4) ease level.

They selected sustenance plus for living wage.

In a paper published by Minimum Wage Fixation Section of ILO it was told to consider three points while fixing living wage : (1) Amount needed for only sustenance, (2) Amount for hygine and modern facilities, (3) Amount needed for easy life/comfort living style.

(iii) Importance. As per the Constitution of International Labour Organisation the workers should get due living wage. That would improve condition of worker and by it peace and prosperity can be established.

In Indian Constitution it has been said that it is responsibility of state to see that labourer gets living wage and it has been told to arrange due system for it. So that by that wage the workers can live easy life according to modern standards and can fully enjoy the joy leisure and all the social and cultural activities.

In India according to opinions of Fair Wage Committee the wage should be sufficient to satisfy the needs of children's education, protection against ill-health, supply of essential things etc. besides satisfying the needs of food, shelter and clothings.

The intention of living wage is to maintain the living standard of labourers. Such wage has been accepted in Australia, U.S.A., New Zealand, Canada and England.

(iv) Limitations. In India it is not possible to give living wage, because in India industries are not able to give living wage to their workers because of less income. In India living wage is the last ideal. In India minimum wage is being insisted and rules are made for minimum wage specially for organised sectors.

(3) Minimum Wage

(i) Definition and Meaning. The minimum wage system is part of the wage policy. There is disparity between salary earning class and non-salary earning class. The income of salary class is very low, while the earning of non-salary class is so high that it defeats salary earners in the market.[2]

The minimum wage is essential for protecting interests of unskilled workers to avoid their possible exploitation and assure them for sustenance. Some factors are being considered while deciding minimum wage. They are known as minimum wage standards. These standards are (1) Living expense, (2) Paying capacity of unit, (3) Productivity of worker.[3] One approach of minimum wage is to link it with economic comfort. So there should be good combination of economic and social comfort in minimum wage.[4]

When we talk about economic comfort it becomes essential to observe paying capacity or economic strength of a firm. It is being argued that employer's paying capacity is limited because he has started business in competitive conditions. So he has to save labour cost.[5] The minimum wage must be practical, effective and acceptable and timely changes, if it is necessary. A study group of National Labour Commission has suggested that minimum wage should be modified within less interval than 5 years.[6]

(ii) Determination Method. In July 1957, 15th National Labour Summit was held. In it important work regarding wage policy was done. It presented concrete concept of minimum wage for the first time. According to its opinion, minimum wage means "need-based minimum wage". Some specifications for determining minimum wage were also discussed in that summit.

The main specifications for minimum wage are as under :

(1) Family of four persons shall be base of minimum wage fixation. The income of other three family members is not to be counted in family of four persons.

(2) Minimum food requirement per Adult is kept 2700 calories.

(3) Need of cloth is kept as 18 metres per person per year.
So, $18 \times 4 = 72$ metres per year.

(4) 20 per cent of minimum wage is spared for fuel, electricity and other miscellaneous expenses.

Thus, it was decided to determine minimum wage according to total of these four expenses. This formula was accepted by Government, Employers and workers. But due to two reasons government could not implement those formula :

(1) This decision was taken by the labour summit not the government.

(2) Government do not have time to execute the administration for implementation of recommendation.[7]

(iii) Implementation in India. All state governments implement the minimum wage law recommended by wage board within the framework of directive policies and ideology. The wage laws are followed in different zones for the workers of different sectors. District minimum wage supervisor's office observes for the implementation and takes action if complain of improper implementation of law comes from workers.

(iv) Importance. Minimum wage is very important matter. It is a matter of human injustice and politically fatal matter that a part of population earns almost nothing.[8] The minimum wage improves living standard of workers, increase their purchasing power, boosts up economic development by measuring production. It also increases productivity of the workers.[9]

(v) Limitations. There are some limitations in determining minimum wage such as to decide base year, to estimate needs of workers and paying capacity of employers and there are also differences regarding the calory-wise need of food for workers. There are opinions between 2000 to 3500 calories. Similarly various estimates have been made regarding needs of clothings and shelter. Besides this there are problems to arrange due system for determining and implementing the minimum wage.

It is also argued that it is not proper and judicious to give equal minimum wage to the workers with different skill.

All states of India were instructed to form wage laws up to 15 March 1950. But they were not formed even in 1960. Finally it was formed in 1974, but there are still many anomalies in it. This law is not being implemented in many industries and sectors. So workers in isolated sectors, do not get advantage of it.

4. Real Wages and Monetary Wages

(i) Meaning. The wage which is paid in the form of monetary terms or in the terms of national currency is monetary wage. But how much he can purchase from that money and other benefits except the wages that matter is known by real wage. It can be said that real wage is available in less proportion if increase in monetary wage is less than increase in the prices.

(ii) Importance. It has been a topic of deep interest to study the trends of real wage and income of industrial workers during the planning time.[10] But it has drawn less attention of researches. A remarkable effort has been made in this direction in a report of National Labour Organisation.[11] A remarkable team appointed by Reserve Bank of India to study income, wage and price policy has told that "The main purpose of income policy is to link the huge structure of monetary income generation with the social purposes of the plan."[12] Practically price level must be invariably considered while forming the wage policy.

The object of the category of the employment should be the need of social justice and income generation for the future development.[13]

It is very essential that the productivity of workers should increase to increase the production in the nation. So it is essential to consider the real wage besides monetary wage.

As said in the First Five Year Plan the growth rate is decided not according to only needs of workers but also according to needs of sources of the nation.[14]

In Third Plan it is said that workers get advantage only by increase in productivity.[15] So concept of real income is very important.

(iii) In India. In India there has been increase in the monetary income of the workers during the planning period. But as the increase in the prices are more than the increase in the income, the real wage has not increased as much as monetary wages. Except First Five Year Plan there has been decrease in real wage compared to monetary wage.

The workers of the organised sectors get increase in monetary wage with the increase in price index. But the workers of unorganised sectors do not get such increase in the wage.

REFERENCES

1. Govt. of India Ministry of Labour, *Report of the Committee on Fair Wages*, Manager of Publications, Delhi, 1949.
2. Palekar, S.A., *Problems for Wage Policy for Economic Development*, pp. 201-203.
3. International Labour Organisation, *Minimum Wage in Latin America*, pp. 16-17.
4. —, *Problems of Wage Policy in Asian Countries*, Geneva, 1956, pp. 75-76.
5. —,"Wage fair wages clauses in public contracts", *Report of Thirty first Session*, Geneva, 1948."
6. National Commission of Labour, "Report of the study group of construction Industry", Manager of Pub., Delhi, 1968, p. 23.
7. Pokanathan, P.S., "Problems and wages and wage fixation", In Labour and Planning (ed.) by Radha Kamal Mukerjee, Pub. 1964, pp. 232-233.
8. I.L.O, *Minimum Wages in Latin America Studies and Reports*, New series No. 34, Geneva, 1954, p. 3.
9. *Ibid.*, p. 16.

10. Madan, B.K., "The Real Wages of Industrial Labour in India", *Management Development Institute*, New Delhi, 1972, p. 11.
11. Palekar, S.A., *Problems of Wage Policy for Economic Development*, Asia Pub. House, Bombay.
12. R.B.I., *Report on a Framework for Income and Price Policies*, Bombay, 1967, p. 67.
13. Government of India, *National Commission of Labour Report*, 1969, Para., 15-26, p. 227.
14. Government of India, *First Five Year Plan*, p. 571.
15. Government of India, *Third Five Year Plan*, p. 261.

4

Wage Structure, Labour Market and Wage Differentiation

> There are three main segments of labour market. *viz.*, Demand of labour, Supply of labour and Wage determination. The main function of labour market is to co-ordinate work and workman. And to fix wages, in such a manner that quality and quantum of labour may be maintained.
>
> —*T.S. Papola*

Outline of Chapter

1. Wage Structure
   (1) Definition, segments and form of wage.
   (2) Meaning and importance of wage structure.
   (3) Inter-industrial wage structure.
2. Labour Market
   (1) Classical approach.
   (2) Neo-classical approach.
   (3) Structural approach.
   (4) Multidimensional labour market.
   (5) Co-ordinative approach.
   (6) Local labour market.
3. Wage Differentiation
   (1) Meaning and definition
   (2) Explanation
   (3) Function of wage differentiation and factors effecting it.
   (4) Regional factors

(5) Kinds of wage differentiation.

(6) Evaluation.

1. WAGE STRUCTURE

(1) Definition, Segments and Form of Wage

It is necessary to understand of wage, before studying wage structure. According to the payment of Wages Act 1936, the wage means all type of remuneration (salary, allowances etc.) which is reflected in the monetary form, which is a part of job, and it is given in the return of service of a person. Following segments are included in it :

(a) Remuneration, payable according to court order, or as per agreement of parties.

(b) Remuneration payable during overtime or holidays.

(c) Additional remuneration, as per service condition (it can be said bonus, or any name).

(d) The sum payable at the end of the service, which has been decided by law, contract or other means. It may be including deduction or excluding deduction. There is no stipulated time for payment.

(e) Sum payable to the employee according to various schemes, which existed at that time.

Following matters are not included wage :

1. The sum which is not payable according to do court order in which bonus is not decided, or as per service condition this amount is not decided.
2. The matters except included in the wages as per general order or special order of state government, which includes residential facilities, electricity, water and other facilities.
3. Any share or provident fund or its interest paid by employers to his employee.
4. Any travelling allowance or expense of travel relief.
5. The sum of payment for the expenses done for a person due to the nature of the service.
6. Sum of gratuity, after the end of service/retirement. Thus wage involves allowances, leave encashment etc. but does not include provident fund contribution or housing allowances etc.

Thus wage is a broad concept which includes many factors. So, it can be said that wage is total of various segments. Following matters are included in wage :

1. Basic Pay

2. Cash allowances, including dearness allowance, production bonus, efficiency bonus and other allowances.
3. Monetary reliefs.
4. Profit-based annual bonus.
5. Arrears.

In fact, in law of 1936, concession, has been not included in wage. But reference to broad interpretation they are included in wages.

(2) Meaning and Importance of Wage Structure

The wage is a prime factor, effecting status and living standard of workman. It also effects production cost. So, it is very important to determine properly.

The mass or summation of various wage rates is wage structure. It may be relative wage, prevailing in plant or industry. It includes various wage rates, in various industries which are interlinked with each other. The wage difference observed in one profession or industry or professions or industries. The mass summation of all these wage rates is wage structure.

The wage structure is very important, with reference to place and time. The wage structure of plant or industries of various places or time can be known by it.

All types of income can be connected by equality and difference methods where there is efficient economy and all factors including labour are active in context to industries. Traditions, laws, etc. factors play vital role in wage determination, but these factors are also highly effected by market trends.

The wage structure divides various industries and professions, by mode of wage. So workman of same category, receive different wage. So difference is seen in the wages unskilled workmen of organised industries and non-organised industries.

The wage structure is seen to be defective, unbalanced and incomplete. And it is even unsatisfactory, if we observe wage level and changes in it. It can be clearly seen that the real wage does not increase with money wage.

(3) Inter-industrial Wage Structure

According to the hypothesis of neo-classical economists, in the long run there shall be trends of same wage-rate fixation if workmen shall proceed from low wage market to high wage market. It is stated that the wage fixing institutes have created incompetency, but they have given hopes for equal rate. Contrary to that it is said that comparative factors and scope and methods of industries have created wage structure with broad wage differences. Some experts have tried to connect wage structure with broad wage differences. Some experts have tried to connect wage structure with economic development and they have recommended to present theory of wage in context to economic development. They are Dunlop Roathbaum (1955), Reynolds Taft (1955), Turner (1966) etc.

Johri and Agrawal (1960), Sohni (1969), Varma (1971), Papola (1972) and Dholakiya made study between 1950 and 1964. In this study discussion regarding inter-industrial wage structure was done. According to this study, immobility and convertibility, these two characteristics are observed in industrial wage structure.

In this study the role of market factors like profitability, productivity, density of capital, part of wage in price etc. in inter-industrial wage difference, has been explained.

We assume that factors like capital density, productivity of labour, part of wage in price rise etc., factors effect inter-industrial wage differences considering this matter, we can explain modes of inter-industrial wage structure like this :

$$W = \alpha + \beta_1 k + \beta_2 v + \beta_3 W/V + e$$

The interpretation of the segments of the model is as under:

W = per worker, annual wage

k = Fix capital per worker

v = Net price rise per worker

w/v = Share of wages in value added

α = Constant

$\beta1$, $\beta2$, $\beta3$ = Regression index number

e = Error terms.

According to this model, the main factors effecting wage structure are density of capital, share of wages in value added, net value added by labourers etc.

2. LABOUR MARKET

The whole wage structure has come in existence due to Labour Market Factors and it changes also by it. So it is essential to study labour market.

Labour market is an important factor in modern economy. It presents, inter-process of various kinds of demand and supply of labour. Previously it was considered like other commodity market. But economists after Keynes, considered it different and analyzed it.

There are three factors of labour market : supply of labour, demand of labour and wage determination. The main task of labour market is to co-ordinate work and workers. And to determine wage in such a manner that proportion and quality of the supply of labour may be maintained.[1]

(1) Classical Approach

Classical Economists believed that distribution is being done, according to general rule of distribution.[2] The wage is decided according to demand and supply of labour just like price of other commodity is fixed as per its demand and supply. In short period supply remains steady, so wage is changed according to demand. They also stated that wage is fixed on the basis of wage fund. Explanation of wage was given to the possibility of factor substitution. In the long run with reference to hypothesis of perfect competition, they also explained about wage differentiation. Adam Smith[3] told about wage differentiation caused by non-economic factors. These factors include cleanliness, strictness, dirtyness, success, etc. Marshall told that unemployment indicates permanent labour surplus than demand of labour.[4] Hicks says that labour market is rarely in equilibrium.[5]

(2) Neo-Classical Approach

These economists have criticized approach of competition.

These economists have concentrated on labour market process, which includes individual employee and firm; and individual labour and function of his unions.[6]

Javons, Mangers, Volras, etc., presented regarding labour market by constant, micro-oriented, economic analysis. Marshall and Hicks gave remarkable explanation regarding wages. Thus neo-classical economists presented approach of economic development with context to general equilibrium in steady framework.[7] These economists talked about substitution of factors and wages in marginal productivity.

According to these economists, in the short period, wage changes. But, in long run, coordination and combination of productive labour and capital shall decide the maximum limitation of profit.

The neo-classic economists explained wages on the basis of marginal productivity. But, marginal productivity cannot be measured.

The thoughts of neo-classicals are not observed practically, in agriculture also.[8] Labour recruitment in industrial sector and wage determination process have their own reasons. Its effects are observed on labour market. There is no sound co-ordination between them.[9] From the incomplete information regarding efficiency of labourers, it is found that firms do not follow prices.[10] Gunnar Myrdal has commented that human element has been neglected in classical and neo-clsssical approaches.[11] It is the main limit of neo-classical approach that it has driven out supply function from analysis system.[12]

(3) Structural Approach

Reynolds studied American labour market, in which use of social approach, in labour market was started.[13] Other economists also follow his approach while giving explanation of labour market. Reynolds told that demand of labour is connected with choice of employer and not with the quality of labourer's productivity.[14] It has been known that the employer has his own standards to decide quality of his wokers.[15] Thus, demand of labour of a firm is not connected with technology or expense factors, but it is connected with institutional factors. Similarly decision of supply of labour is also effected by institutional factor. The activity of a person is decided by traditions and institutions and not the economic factors. The wage rate effects positively to those, who are out of labour market. But for those who are in the labour market for them wage rate may effect positively or may not act positive.[16] The workers have no information regarding wages of other firms. So they can not compare other allowances with wages.[17] The workers have not stayed among companies. So they cannot do comparison between companies and they accept the whichever work they get first.[18] The labourers have their own concepts regarding "job satisfaction" with reference to their own economical and social status, education and training. So, considering this matter, voluntary mobility is observed among them. Those who have got job satisfaction they do not move.[19] Voluntary mobility increases with the increase in age.[20]

(4) Multidimensional Labour Market

The labour market is multidimensional. It has many peculiarities. In this market, the labourer is not influenced by factors of competition. The competition power become limited. So worker is unable to achieve benefits even if wage increases. The local labour market is a market with a speciality. Kerr[21] says that local labour market is a natural labour market which is different form. It is different than recognised market sector. Thus labour market is not only medium of wage determination, but it is a unit being effected by institutional factors. That is why it is said that employment market is not merely unit presenting the minimum and maximum limitation of wage fixation. Generally one price exists in it. But it is not due to market transactions but it is due to policy.[22]

(5) Co-ordinative Approach

Some experts have tried to explain labour market by co-ordination opinions, of colonialists and neo-classicals. The effort has been made to solve the problems of colonialists, within the neo-classic framework. The labour supply is result of a family decision and it is connected with consumption behaviour.[23] In this reference, the theory of human capital formation has been presented. According to it, current and past human capital formation is co-ordinated. And from it, the decision is being taken that how much wage should be fixed at the certain stage of worker's life cycle.[24]

Wage structure is effected by many factors. Some economists give more importance to economic factors than non-economic factors. These economists include Phels (1970)[25], Charles and McClaurine (1943)[26], Hunter and Reid (1972)[27], Mackan (1971)[28], Walter (1962)[29] etc.

(6) Local Labour Market

The wage structure of Indian labour market is mainly effected by local factors. Thus, even though, wage structure is effected by local factors.

Nothing specific has been said regarding efforts of local labour market on wage structure. So it is said that, we know better about lunar surface, than what we know about process of local labour market.[30] The definition of local labour market can be given with context to visit of various places, for work, remaining within the limit of certain area.[31] In such area, it is not essential to change residence even if the place of job changes.[32] Local situations and factors effect local labour market's wage structure.

Due to unemployment of agricultural labourers rigidity is observed in local labour market and particularly in rural labour market. Here it is observed that there is no significant effect on supply of labour, even though wage rate changes.

In rural labour market more labour surplus is observed which is used at a certain time.[33] The labourers are willing to work at any rate. There are differences in supply and potential supply, among these areas. But there are no difference in wages due to these differences. In rural labour market this peculiarity is very important.[34]

Social tradition and family institute clinch the person with his residence. So labour supply shall be more localized. So wage equality cannot be achieved, by competitive factors.

In rural area, all agricultural labourers do not get job in agricultural sector. In rural labour market also they get very few employment in non-agriculture sector.

In developed countries, it has been observed that women participation in labour force is positive function with reference to wage rate. But it is a negative function, considering family income.[35] If family income increases, than women participation in labour force decreases. But if women participation increases, family income increases.

Thus, women labour supply line is backward sloping. Thus, participation of women in labour force of rural labour market depends on family income. Women labour supply is not effected by wage rate.

Thus, wage structure is effected by local factors of local labour market.

3. WAGE DIFFERENTIATION

(1) Meaning and Definition

Large scale wage differentiations can be observed if we study wage structure. They are of different types. The wage differences means difference in wages, according to area, region skill, season sex etc. The difference in the cost of labour is caused to inequality in the skill of labour force, limited competition in commodity market and speedy technical changes. But in the long run, cost of labour becomes equal due to competition, that belief does not seem to be true. The hypothesis of classical economist is unrealistic that units of labour have same property (homogeneous).

For the theoretical discussion of labour market and explanation of wage determination, not the similar but group of different wage rate-oriented wage structure is essential.[36]

In modern period, inter-professional mobility becomes difficult. So wage differentiation is observed in various professions and trade, in even short period. The wage differentiations are eliminated in the long run and tendency of becoming equal wage, takes place is not the right concept.

(2) Explanation

The wage differentiations and variation in the labour cost, for various purposes, is observed in the labour market due to limited competition, rapid technological changes, and skill difference in the labour force.[37]

The worker does not migrate, only considering the wages. But his voluntary mobility depends, rather on, difference of available work, their wage differences.[38]

Many studies[39] have been made, regarding wage differentiations in which, supply-oriented factors, geographical factors, other benefits except wages etc. matters were examined. Marshall tried to explain the concept of wage differenciation, with reference to quality of labour, by the concept of efficient earning. In recent studies, concept of local labour market, was studied with reference to wage and quality of labourer.

The skill or quality of worker is a prime factor affecting wage differences.

The wage difference comes in existence, due to difference in quality. Labourers can be decided in 7 sections *viz* : more skilled, most skilled, skilled, semi-skilled, unskilled, more unskilled and most unskilled. All these workers get different wages.

The study of Lester examined the wage differences, with reference to quality.[40] Reynolds also believe that wage differences is basically, difference in the quality.

The quality of low wage earners is also low. It has been also observed that workers of the big firms, get more wage than workers of the small firm. Of course there is no base after this theory.[41] Some studies indicates that the wage differences depend on profitability or paying capacity.

The firm with monopoly, in the market gives more wage to its workers. While firm which has to face competition, they give low wage to their workers.[42]

(3) Functions of Wage Differentiation and Factors Effecting it

There are three main functions of wage differentiation:[43]

1. It gives inspirations to work in the fields, where there is more demand, which are more risky, income is more uncertain and chances of unemployments are more.
2. It gives inspirations to the youths for more education and training. It also encourage labourers to improve their skill and efficiency to get higher wages.
3. It decides the social status of workers. The wage differences on the basis of skill or profession give information to evaluate the function of workers. Thus, wage differences are vital matter for firms and labour market. A firm should consider certain matters while forming wage structure, with differences. According to fair wage committee following matters should be considered while deciding the wage differences. Training, category of skill, workload, participation of experience, proportion of responsibility, risk and possibilities of accidents in the work, physical and mental needs problems caused by disease due to duty etc.

The National Council of Applied Economic Research made a study with reference to Indian Industries[44] in which factors effecting wage differences were studied. The wage differences are effected by administrative factors, structure of technology and production process. It is a main problem, in connection with the wage problem that what should be the minimum and maximum proportion of wages. The representatives of INTUC has said that it should not be more than 1 : 8, while A.I.T.U.C. has suggested it 1 : 4. It has made suggestions to the Sugar Wage Board that a semi-skilled worker should get 25 per cent more wage than unskilled worker, skilled worker should get 50 per cent more and most skilled worker should get 100 per cent than unskilled worker.

(4) Regional Factors

The regional or geographical factors also affect the wage differences. They also depend on the form and working pattern of national economy.[45] Due to some regional factors the power of competitive factor becomes limited which causes certain problems. In this situation sometimes wage differences create improper unequality which badly effects the work.[46] The study of wage differences is vital, to study the wage structure of underdeveloped nations in context to low wage rate.[47] In some studies large geographical wage differences are observed.[48] India is also a underdeveloped country too. So in India also widespread wage differentiation in Industries are observed.[49] Thus, study conducted in India also support this theory.[50]

Thus, the concepts of wage differentiation is vital for workers, employers, firms, labour market and whole economy.

(5) Kinds of Wage differentiation

1. Skill-based wage differences. As discussed above, the quality of work is important factor in the wage differences. The difference in wages is due to difference in the quality of work. The employer wishes to pay according to the marginal productivity of workers. The skilled workers get high wage due to their high marginal productivity, while unskilled or semi-skilled workers have less marginal productivity. So they get low wage.

2. Regional wage differences. As discussed above, the wage depends on regional factors. So there is difference in the wages urban and rural workers. Same way there are different wages in different cities and villages.

3. Gender-based wage differences. Nowadays women also work in various fields and sectors. Many studies have been made regarding their functions and wage. According to J.S. Mill (1969)[51] women should have capacity to earn according to their feminine status. The men-women equality has no sense if the women are not economically independent. Of course in some sectors they have reached at a stage where they can compete with men.

According to Boserup (1970)[52] women can be observed as competitor of men in offices, industries and general unskilled jobs. Yet, they get less wage than men. According to the study of Cante[53] in U.S.A. the women with same equalisations were getting only 3/4 wage of men. In a study in England it was observed that average income of women was 80 per cent of that of men.[54]

In Canada the average income of women was 78 per cent of that of the men.[55] In Israel the illiterate women earns 40 per cent of that of the men and literate women's share is 46 per cent to 60 per cent. In Thiland[56] women are far behind in all income levels.[57] In Japan women belong to age group of 40-49 years get only 64 per cent of wage than the men of the same age group. In China also there is disparity in the wages of man and woman.[58] The study of Ryan and Ghodke (1990)[59] says that in 1975-76, the wage of women was 50 per cent less than that of men. Subramaniam says that wage differentiations between men and women are kept intentionally,[60] by which women get lower wage even than traditional wage. In 1969, it was told that women get employment only due to their lower rate.[61] And they shall loose jobs if their wages are made equal to the men. But this concept cannot be accepted on the ground of equality and justice.

In India article 16 (1) of the Constitution insists for equal job opportunity. Article 16(2) says to eliminate the differences of religion, caste, community and sexual differences. Section 30 of the Directive Principles has recommended for equal right to get opportunity or sustenance and equal wage for equal work, for men, women and children. In this connection only the Government of India has made a law in 1975 for "Equal wage for equal work."

The concept of equal wage for men and women is very important concept. The participation rate of women in labour force of India and world is remarkable.

According to the report of Planning Commission in India participation of women in labour force is 28 per cent, in U.S.A. it is 32 per cent, in Asia it is 34 per cent, in North America it is 38 per cent, in Europe it is 37 per cent, and in Russia it is 49 per cent. Thus, instead of their remarkable participation the women are being given less wage than men.

According to the opinion of a committee appointed by the

Government, the principle of "equal wage for equal work" is not being implemented. This concept is imaginatory. In most of the industries women are given low wage. It has been argued by an expert named Stevenson that women get low wage because they have concentrated on low wage jobs.[62]

4. Growth-oriented wage differentiations. Differentiations in wages can be observed on the basis of the development. Different wages are observed in developed and underdeveloped areas. High wage is given in developed urban area and developed rural area. While in underdeveloped rural area and underdeveloped urban area low wage is prevailing. Similarly there are low wages in undeveloped nations compared to the developed nations.

5. Seasonal Wage Differences. The worker working in the seasonal sector like agriculture construction etc., they get wages according to the season. In such professions workers get high wages during the season. But, they get less wage in off season.

6. Work-based Wage Differentiations. The different workers are getting different wages, for different functions. There are many functions in one profession. These functions are performed by skilled and unskilled workers. Even there are different work for skilled workers. Thus, workers are being given different wages for different types of work.

(6) Evaluation

There are many differentiations in the wages of workers due to some factors like regional factors, growth-based factors, skill etc. Some differentiations are justified, while some differences are improper and invalid.

The differences on the basis of skill, function, profession, season and area are justified. But differences in the wages of man and women or different caste religion, region cannot be justified . Wage differences for the same cadre workers for the same work is not proper. However, it is not possible to eliminate the wage differences. It is neither advisable nor passible to give equal wage to all workers. However, exploitation of workers due to low wages can be avoided.

REFERENCES

1. Papola, T.S., "*Economics of Labour Market*" in V.B. Singh (ed.), "*Labour Research in India*", Popular, Bombay, 1970, p. 170.
2. Rottenberg, S., "On choice in Labour Market", in J.B.M. Penguin Modern Economics, 1968, p. 52.
3. Adam Smith, *An Enquiry into the Nature and Causes of the Wealth of Nations, Modern Library Edition*, Random House, New York, 1937.

4. Quoted by A.V. Raman Rao in his Collection of "Essays on Indian Labour", Popular, Bombay, 1965, p. 299.
5. Hicks, J.R., *Theory of Wages*, Macmillan, London, 1932, p. 76.
6. Dale Yoder and H.G. Heneman, Jr., *Labour Economics and Industrial Relations*, Southwest Publication Co., Chicageo, 1959, p. 488.
7. Marti Blauge, *Economic Theory in Retrospect*, Vikas Pub., New Delhi, 1983, p. 312.
8. Loyed Fisher, "The Harvest Labour Market in California", *Quarterly Journal of Economics*, Vol. LXV, Nov. 1951, pp. 463-491.
9. Lester, E.A., *Economics of Labour* (ed.), Macmillan, London, 1964, p. 267.
10. Dissarides, C.A., *Labour Market Adjustment : Micro-Economic Foundation of Short-run, Neoclassical and Keynesian Dynamics*, Cambridge University Press, 1976, pp. 26-27.
11. Myrdal, Gunnar., *Asian Drama*, Vol. II; Part V. ch. 21, Lanthon, New York, 1968, p. 987.
12. Dunlop, J.T., "The Task of Contemporary Wage Theory", in Ray Marshall and Richard Perlman (ed.), *An Anthropology of Labour Economics*, John Wiley, New York, 1972, p. 219.
13. Blackburn, R.M., and Michel Mann, *The Working Class in Labour Market*, Macmillan, London, 1979, p. 4.
14. Reynolds, L., *The Structure of Labour Market*, Harper, New York, 1951, p. 85.
15. Ress, A.J. and G.P. Shultz, *Workers and Wages in Urban Labour Market*, Chicago Uni. Press, Chicago, 1970, p. 220.
16. Standing, G., *Labour Force Development*, ILO, 1978, p. 56.
17. Reynolds, L.S., "The Supply of Labour to the Firm", *Quarterly Journal of Economics*, May 1946, Vol. LX, pp. 390-411.
18. Martin and Fryer, Quoted by W.R.M. Blackburn and Michael Mann, "The Working Class in the Labour Market", Macmillan, London, 1979, p. 138.
19. Reynolds, L.G. and J. Shister, *Job Horizans : A Study of Job Satisfaction and Labour Mobility*, Harper, New York, 1949, pp. 108-109.
20. Kreps, *et al.*, *Contemporary Labour Economies : Issues, Analyses and Policies*, Wordsworth Publication, California, 1974, p. 34.
21. Clark, Kerr, "Balkanization of Labour Markets" in E.W. Bakke, Ed., Labour Mobility and Economic Opportunity, Technology Press, 1954, p. 92.
22. ——, "Wage-Relationships : Comparative Impact of Market and Power Forces" in J.T. Dunlop (ed.), *The Theory of Wage Determination*, Macmillan, London, 1964, pp. 173-193.
23. Backer, G.S., "Theory of Allocation of Time", *Economic Journal*, 1965, pp. 473-517.
24. ——, *Human Capital* (ed.), Columbia Uni. Press, New York 1975, pp. 29-30.
25. Phels, E.S., *Micro-Economics Foundations of Employment and Inflation Theory*, New York, 1970.
26. Charles, A. Myers and W.R. Maclaurine, *The Movement of Factory Workers*, The Technology Press, London, 1943.
27. Hunter, L.C. and G. Reid, *Urban Worker Mobility*, OECD, Paris, 1968.
28. Mackan, D.L, *Labour Market Under Different Employment Conditions*, Allen & Unwin, 1971, pp. 124-125.
29. Walter O.I., "Labour as a Quasi Fix Factor", *Journal of Political Economy*, December, 1963.

30. Robinson, Devek, "Myths of Local Labour Market", *Journal of the Institute of Personnel Management*, Vol. 1, 1967-68, p. 36.
31. Goodman, "Conceptual and Methodological Problems in the Research on the Local Labour Market", *British Journal of Industrial Relations*, July, 1974.
32. Reynolds, L.G., *op. cit.*
33. Ladjinsky, W., "The Green Revolution in Punjab : A Field Trip", *Economic and Political Weekly*, Vol. IV, No. 26, June, 28, 1969.
34. Papola, T.S., "The Indian Labour Market", *Economic and Political Weekly*, Vol. III, No. 30, 1968.
35. Standing, G., *Labour Force Participation and Development*, International Labour office, Geneva, 1978, p. 75.
36. Cf. Dunlop, J.T., "The Task of Contemporary Wage Theory", in his (ed.), *The Theory of Wage Differentiation*, Macmillan, London, 1964, p. 15.
37. Papola, T.S., "Wage Differentials and Competition in the Labour Market", *Indian Journal of Labour*, Vol, XVIII, April-July, 1974, No.1-2, pp. 30-56.
38. Dunlop, J.T., *Ibid.*, p. 15.
39. Reynolds, Llyod, *The Structure of Labour Markets*, Hamper and Brathers, New York, 1951, p. 3.
40. Lester, R.S., "A Range Theory of Wage Differentials" *Industrial and Labour Relation Review*, 5, July, 1952, pp. 487-488.
41. Albert, A., New Measures of Wage Earning Compensation in Manufacturing, New York, National Bureau of Economic Research, 1960.
42. Lester, R.A. "Size of Establishment Compensation Differentials", *Industrial Relation*, October 1967.
43. Sinha, P.R.N., *Wage Determination*, p. 172.
44. Patel, B.B., "Structure of Inter-district, Inter-sectoral and Int.-Ind Wage Differentiation."
45. Turen, H.A., "Wage Trends, Wage Policies and Collective Bargaining : Problems of Underdeveloped Countries", Cambridge Uni. Press, 1965, p. 61.
46. Sardamani, K., "Inter-State Differences in Manufacturing Workers Earning, A Study in Money and Real Wages", *Economic and Political Weekly*, May 2, 1970. Vol. V, No. 18.
47. Gadgil, D.R., *Wage Regulation and Other Problems of Industrial Labour in India*, Bombay, 1942.
48. Sardamani, K., "Inter-state Differences in Manufacturing Workers Earning, A Case Study in Money and Real Wages", *Economics and Political Weekly*, May 2, 1970.
49. Swaney, P.K., "Inter-Industry Wage Differentials in India", *The Indian Economic Journal*, July-Sept. 1969, Vol. XVII, No. 1.
50. Papola T.S., and V.P. Bhardwaj, "Dynamics of Inter-Industry Wage Structure, An Inter-country Analyses", *The Economic Journal*, March 1990, Vol. XXX.
51. Mill, J.S., *The Subjugation of Women*, London, 1869.
52. Boserup, E., *Womens Role in Economic Development*, George Allen and Unwin, 1970.
53. Cante, M., *Labour Market Discrimination Against Women in 5000 American Families*, Vol. 4, University of Michigan.
54. Chipline, B. and Sleane, P.L.J., *Sex Discrimination in Labour Market*, Macmillan Press, London, 1976.
55. Gunderson, M., "Male-Female Wage Differentials and the Impact of Equal Pay Legislation", *The Review of Economic and Statistics*, 46, 1975, pp. 462-469.

56. Klinovo, Malud, "Profitability in Investment in Education in Israel", Marice Folk, Institute of Economic Research in Israel, 1966.

57. Blaug, M., "Rates of Returns to Investment in Education in Thiland: A Survey", Mimeo, National Council of Education, Thiland, 1971.

58. Gupta, K.P., "Emancipation and Enslavement : The Confusion and Communist Variation", *In Woman of the Worked*, Ed. Phodins, U. and Malini, I., Vikas Publishing House, 1978.

59. Ryan, J.G. and R.D. Ghodke, "Labour Market Behaviour in Rural Villages of South India : Effects of Season, Sex and Socio-Economic Status", Working Paper, *ICRISAT*, 1970.

60. Subramaniam, M.K., *Wage in India*, Mcgraw Hill Book Co. 1977.

61. Government of India, *Report of the National Commission on Labour*, 1979.

62. Stevenson, M., "Women's Wages and Job Segmentation" (ed.), Edwards, R. Reichi, M. and Gordon, N.M., Lexington Books, 1975.

5

Wage Policy in India

> "The level of wages, both money and real, closely influences and is affected by the actual unemployment with which these economies are now plauged."
>
> —*A.J. Fonseka*

Outline of Chapter

1. Introduction
2. Meaning of Wages and Wage Policy
3. Importance and Objectives of Wage Policy
4. Needs of Integrated Proper Wage Policy
5. Issues of Wage Policy
6. Formation of Integrated Wage Policy
7. Conclusion

1. INTRODUCTION

There are very serious problems of unorganised labourers. But problems of very lower wages with very less employment is a crucial problem of labourers engaged in unorganised sector. They do not get proper wages and at the same time do not get proper employment opportunities. Lower wage rate is a direct result of huge unemployment and underemployment. "... The level of wages both money and real, closely influences and is affected by the actual unemployment with which these economies are now plagued. A significant cause of this high rate of unemployment, particularly in urban areas is often claimed to be the high level of wages which is denounced as unjustifiable and against the national interest."[1] Herberger observed that the annual earnings of casual construction workers, household sweepers and rickshaw drivers in major Indian cities are about double those of landless agricultural workers in the rural areas. This influences the decision of the rural wage earners to migrate to the towns in search of employment.[2]

Due to large surplus of unskilled and semi-skilled labourers, it is very natural for wage earners to offer very low labour supply price of their labour for subsidence purpose.

Wage is only a single source of wage earner for livelihood. Wage policy can directly effect on wages. It also effected on cost of production and price level. But unfortunately, there is no proper, perfect and integrated wage policy as such. Because there are many issues on the way of such type of wage policy.

2. MEANING OF WAGES AND WAGE POLICY

According to Wage Payment Act, 1936, wage is expressed in monetary terms and reward for productive labour work, it is responsibility of employer. It includes the following :

1. Payment mutually agreed upon by both parties or as in the Court Judgement.
2. Payment towards the level or overtime by an employee.
3. According to the terms and conditions of service extra or special payment payable, *i.e.* bonus.
4. Payment at the time of leaving the job as specified by contract, law or rules.
5. Payment towards the employee as right during his service.

The policy either deciding or affecting on such type of wages can be defied as wage policy. In the formation of wage policy, Central and State Governments, Wage Commissions, wage Boards, Pay Commissions, Wage Committee and sub-committees can play an important role.

3. IMPORTANCE AND OBJECTIVES OF WAGE POLICY

Wage policy is an important tool of economic and social security for unorganised labourers. It accelerates the overall development process. Wage policy directly affected on production and productivity of goods and services in the country. It also decides the pattern of investment.

There are several crucial important aims of wage policy. Some of them can be briefly noted as under :

1. To increase production and productivity through raising efficiency, skills, productivity and competitiveness of workers.
2. To eliminate exploitation of the workers by protecting their wages.
3. According to V.V. Giri, the labourers should obtain higher wage which is affordable for owners, it should also increase efficiency, productivity and production.
4. According to ILO[3], wage policy should fulfil the basic needs of labourers, to protect labourers by formatting and implementing

minimum wages, straightening the bargaining power of labour unions, protecting labour class against inflationary pressure, affordable for owners.

4. NEEDS OF INTEGRATED PROPER WAGE POLICY

There is an urgent need of proper, perfect, practical and well organised and integrated wage policy in India. It is needed for protecting unorganised labourers which is ninety per cent of total labour force. Aims of wage policy and five year plans are likely to equal or same. For materialise these objectives, there is a need of proper wage policy. Less wages is one important cause of poverty, malnutrition and undernutrition. This can be eliminated by proper wage policy.

Proper, perfect and integrated policy is also needed for removing drawbacks of wage structure, wage payment and unjustifiable wage differentiations. It is helpful for maintaining industrial peace. There are serious human problems arised from implementation of new economic reforms. These can be solved by formating and implementing proper wage policy.

5. ISSUES OF WAGE-POLICY

As mentioned earlier, there is no proper, perfect, well integrated wage policy as such. Because there are various issues, hurdles, in formating and implementing such type of wage policy.

1. Rigid, Complex and Localised Labour Market

Labour market is the procedure of dividing/distributing in some basic groups and thereby deciding their value. For this, the demand and supply of labour and its value of labour to consider in this labour market. And the inter-relationship between these three is also considered and gone through.[4]

Commodities market can be regional, national and international but labour market is more determined by the regional factors. It is also affected by social, personal, economic, cultural factors and so many other things and problems.

Local labour market do possess some specific characteristics and due to these characteristics no one can judge or predict the trends and outlook of the labour market. We can say more about the surface of moon than the outlook of local labour market.[5] Workers do prefer to work in some personally and predefined boundaries, and the definition of labour market can be given with that respect.[6]

Due to localised factors in labour market, several problems of wages and wage structures are arised. The difference in the wages of different profession and business is reflected by wage structure.[7] The factors of demand and supply of labour cannot work freely, naturally and smoothly in this type of complicated localised labour market.

2. Overpopulation and Surplus Labour Force

India have a huge population and therefore large size of labour force. Until the surplus labour force of underdeveloped countries like India, is not engaged in other industrial activity the workers of rural sector will get lower wages. Because of these two division will come into existence, one is modern sector and other is rural traditional sector.[8] When the population of a country is very large they can be provided employment with low wage rate. When the level of surplus labour force is big the result is in very lower wage rate.

3. Differences in Wages and Employment Opportunities

Wage differences are evident due to competition and technological changes which has changed the skilled and value for work.[9] To understand the labour market condition, it is desired to have a more context system of wage rates.[10] Worker does not move here and there due to the difference in wage rates, he moves because of the change in the available work.[11]

In the modern method of research more emphasis is given to physical working condition and supply of workers.[12] But their trends are very different. Differences in wages is basic issue of wage policy. According to the study of Dr. B.B. Patel, wage differentiation is based on system and nature of work of region or country. According to another study due to regional factors strength of competitive elements becomes limited. Then it would create some problems. When competitive elements are not working well, wage differentiation creates irrational, improper imbalances. This would be badly affected to the functioning of labour market.

There are very wide differences in employment opportunities. It has ever changed and never static. There are large ups and down. This is a great hurdle of effective wage policy.

4. Gender-oriented Wage employment Differentiation

In India the rate of labour participation of female is very lower. Most of the female workers engaged in unorganised sector in which their employment and wage rate is very low.

Cante concluded in his study that in U.S.A. the wages of equal qualified women are 3/4'th of male.[13] A study in Britain, find out that average female earning is 84 per cent of male.[14] This is only 78 per cent in Canada.[15] The average earning of illiterate woman is 40 per cent and 40 to 60 per cent for literate woman, compared to male in Israel.[16] The female worker is far behind in each level of age and education compared to male in Thailand.[17] In India there are many laws for male-female equal wage rate for equal work. But this problem is not solved.[18] Ryan and Ghodke have concluded, there are deliberately 50 per cent lower wages of female workers than male workers in six Indian villages in 1975-76.[19]

5. Negligence of Real Wages

That is ideal wage policy which consider monetary and real wages equally. But here we neglect the real wages in our wage policy. We give prime important only and only to monetary wages. Result is that yet there is considerably increasing in monetary wages, real wages remained lower.

Trends of real wages or earnings of industrial workers are become very interesting subject during the plan period.[20] It is observed that this is least considered by scholars and researches. But National Labour Commission had given importance towards this issue.[21] In 1967, the Reserve Bank of India had appointed a committee for study the wages, income and pricing policies. It had stated that main objective of income policy is to connect with large financial income generation structure with social objectives.[22] At the time of formation of wage policy, price level should be considered. The main object of employment level should be necessary of social justice and capital formation for future development.[23]

Higher productivity of labourers is essential for higher production. For this purpose money wage as well as real wage should be equally considered. First Five Year Plan stated that growth rate is not decided from workers necessities but from necessities of factors of production.[24] Third plan also stated that workers would be benefited only by higher productivity.[25]

The concept of real wage is integral and important part of wage policy, which is neglected, during the plan period. Monetary income of the workers has increased. But the rate of increasing of income is quite low compared to rate of increasing of price level. Therefore, real income has not increased compared to money income. Real income lagging very behind than money income. This is very crucial issue of effective well co-ordinated wage policy.

6. Poor Performance and Implementation of Minimum Wages

Minimum wage is the part of functioning of the government's wage policy. Minimum wage rate is the demand of the present day and is desired for the labour force of the country. There is difference between wage earners and salary earners in the urban area. Income of salary earner is very high and they beat the wage earners in the market.[26] To protect the economic welfare of the unorganised and unskilled labour and to remove their exploitation, it is necessary to have minimum wages.

Minimum Wages is the balance of social and economic easiness. Economic easiness includes capacity of a firm or industrial unit to pay.[27]

Minimum wages should be actual, practical and effective. It is necessary that minimum wages should change in balance way. A committee appointed by National Labour Commission on construction activities notes that minimum wages should change more times than the present practice of once in a five year.[28]

On humanitarian ground it is unjustice and politically it is futile that a part of population earns negative amount.[29] A part from the upliftment of living standard of unorganised labour, minimum wages attempts to serve following two purposes :

(i) To speed up the economic development by increasing the purchasing power with employment and production.

(ii) Worker should get reasonable amount by his production.[30]

In all the states, minimum wage Acts are existed but its implementation is poor. Many times minimum wages rates and its laws have been changed but not implemented in desired manner.

National organisation for Unorganised Labour, National Centre for Labour in its conference at New Delhi, in May 1997, has decided to fight for Rs. 125 as minimum wage rate. It was stated in the conference that due to globalisation, poverty has spread its wings wider. There are 30 crore unorganised workers in the country. And about 250 unorganised businesses, in only very few businesses minimum wage rate is being implemented.

6. FORMATION OF INTEGRATED WAGE POLICY

Above all discussion shows that wage problem is basic problem of unorganised labourers. They are getting low wages. Poverty, malnutrition and undernutrition is a result of lower wages. There are laws, rules and legislation regarding wages in general and minimum wages in specific. Wage laws and regulations only protecting organised labourers which are only 10 per cent of total labour force and 3 per cent of total population. There are laws of minimum wages for protecting unorganised labourers which are 90 (ninety) per cent of total labour force. But implementation of legislation of minimum wages is very poor and pitiable. Therefore, unorganised labourers are obtaining very lower wage rates, which is not sufficient for their minimum subsistence.

In these circumstances there is need for integrated, proper and perfect wage policy. Similar type of National Wage Policy is not possible due to localised nature of labour market and differentiation in economic activities. Therefore, Central Government should decide basic guidelines for wage formation. This should be followed by State Governments and organisers of economic acclivities. There should be efficient formation and implementation of minimum wages in whole unorganised sectors.

Following factors should be considered at a time of formation of integrated wage policy :

1. Work environment which includes nature of work, working conditions, likely and uncleanliness, risk-pain in work, fatigue, etc., should be considered.
2. Basic necessities of labour family which includes basic needs, housing, clothing, health, education etc., should be considered in wage policy.
3. It should care of capacity of pay of entrepreneur. ILO also put stress on this.
4. Social objectives also should be considered in the formation of wage policy. Because labour class is integral and important part of society. Wage level should be above of poverty line.
5. Level of economic development, contribution in total production of industry, developmental level of industry and their problems, process, stages and nature of industrialisation, etc., should be also considered.
6. Existed wage rates, wage levels and wage structure are also important in the formation of wage policy
7. The fundamental aim of wage policy is to solve the wage related problems,
8. The aims of wage policy should be same as aims of planning.

7. CONCLUSION

Human factor is important for not only in production process, but in the whole development process. Therefore, interested and well-organised proper, perfect and practical wage policy is needed for protecting economic and social interests of labour class. Central Government should form such types of broad general wage policy and circulated to the states for necessary action. All unorganised sectors should included in minimum wages. It should be revised every year instead of five years.

REFERENCES

1. Fonseka, A.J. (1975), *Wage Issues in a Developing Economy, The Indian Experience*, Oxford University Press, Mumbai, p 2.

2. Herberger, A.C. (1971), "Measuring the Social Opportunity Cost of Labour", *in International Labour Review*, p. 562.
3. ILO (1956), *The Problems of Wage Policy in Asian Countries*, Geneva.
4. Papola, T.S. and K.K. Subramanian (1975), *Wage Structure and Labour Mobility in Local Labour Market*, Popular Prakashan, Mumbai.
5. Robinson, Devek (1967-68), "Myths of Local Labour Market", *Journal of the Institute of Personal Management*, Vol. I, p. 36.
6. Goodman (1970), "Conceptual and Methodological Problems in the Research on the Local Labour Markets", *British Journal of Industrial Relations*, July.
7. Dudeja, V.D. (1979), "Wage Structure", *The Indian Journal of Labour Economics*, Vol. XXI, January, pp. 34-46.
8. Fonseka, A.J. (1975), *Wage Issues in Developing Economy: The Indian Experience*, Oxford University Press, Mumbai, p. 2.
9. Papola, T.S. (1974), "Wage Differentials and Competition in the Labour Market", *Indian Journal of Labour Economics*, Vol. XVII, April-July, No. 1-2, pp. 39-56.
10. Dunlop, J.P. (1964), "The Task of Contemporary Wage Theory", in his (ed.), *Theory of Wage Differentiation*, Macmillan, London, p. 15.
11. Renolds, Liyod (1951), *The Structure of Labour Market. Hamper and Brothers*, New York, p. 3.
12. Albert, R. and G.P. Schultz (1970), *Workers and Wages in Urban Labour Market*, The University of Chicago Press, London, p. 4.
13. Conte, M., *Labour Market Discrimination against Women in 5000 American Families*, Vol. 4, University of Michigan.
14. Chipline, B. and Sleane (1976), *Sex Discrimination in Labour Market*, Macmillan Press, London.
15. Gunderson, M. (1975), "Male-Female Wage Differentiation and the Impact of Equal Pay Legislation", *The Review of Economics and Statistics*, 46, pp. 462-469.
16. Klonobomsluf, T. (1966), *Profitability in Investment in Education in Israel*, Marice Folk Institute of Economic Research in Isreal.
17. Blaug, M. (1971), "Rates and Returns of Investment in Education in Thailand — A Survey", *Mimea, National Council of Education*, in Thailand.
18. Gupta, K.P. (1978), "Manicipation and Enslavement; The confusion and Communist Variations", in (ed.) *Woman of the World*, Phodnis, U., and Malini, I., Vikas Publishing House.
19. Rayan, J.G. and R.D. Ghodke (1980), "Labour Market Behaviour in Rural Villages of South India; Effects of Season, Sex and Socio-Economic Status", *Working Paper*, ICRISAT.
20. Madan, B.K. (1972), *The Real Wages of Industrial Labour in India, Management Development Institute*, New Delhi, April, p. 11.
21. Palekar, S.A. (1962), *Problems of Wage Policy for Economic Development*, Asia Publishing House, Mumbai.
22. Reserve Bank of India, *Report on a Framework for Incomes and Prices Policies*, Mumbai, p. 7.
23. Government of India, *National Commission on Labour Report*, 1969, Para 15.26, p. 227.
24. Government of India, *First Five Year Plan*, p. 571.
25. Government of India, *Third Five Year Plan*, p. 261.

26. Palekar. S.A. (1962), *Problems of Wage Policy for Economic Development, op. cit.*, pp. 201-203.
27. I.L.O. (1956), *Problems of Wage Policy in Asian Countries*, Geneve, pp. 75-76, and also, ILO, *Minimum Wage Fixing Machinery and Related Problems with Special Reference to Developing Countries*, Report VII (i), at Fifty Third Session, 1969, p. 39.
28. National Commission on Labour (1908), *Report of the Study Group for the Construction Industry*, Manager of Publications, Delhi, p. 23.
29. I.L.O. (1954), *Minimum Wages in Latin America : Studies and Reports*, New Series, No. 34, Geneva, p. 3.
30. *Ibid.*, p. 16.

6

Labour Migration

> "History shows the influence of threat of starvation, Political oppression, religious persecution, eviction, a sense of adventure, an urge to make a future a desire to join relatives abroad or to get away from those at home."
>
> —*Mohinder Singh*

Outline of Chapter

1. Introduction.
2. Approach of Labour Migration
3. Rural-Urban Migration.
4. Theoretical Analysis
5. Evil Effects of Migration.
6. Conclusion.

1. INTRODUCTION

Labour Migration is closely associated with the process of economic development. Brainely Thomas (1973)[1] express the view that all sorts of development may lie behind the decisions of individuals or families to leave one country in order to live in other. "History shows the influence of threat of starvation, political oppression, religious persecution, eviction, a sense of adventure, an urge to make a future a desire to join relatives abroad or to get away from those at home."[2] But in India it is a symbol of crucial and serious problems like poverty/unemployment and underemployment, very low wages, starvation, indebtedness, inability of more employment in farm sector etc. which pushed the labourers out from their permanent native place. Indian unorganised labourers are always wondering here and there in search of employment. This will damage the economic, social, educational life of their families. Migration is a multiple problem. Migration is an important cause for the problems of urbanisation, urban unemployment and poverty, slums, pollution. These trends should be stopped. Each and every person of the country should be able to get gainful employment at his native place. For this purpose there is need of development of farm and allied sectors, cottage and agro-based industries, self-employment etc.

2. APPROACH OF LABOUR MIGRATION

The essential character of migration is that it involves a change in place of abode or place of usual residence a taking up of life in a new or different place.[3]

A migrant is defined as a person who has changed his usual place of residence from one politically defined area to another similar area. Thus, the concept of migration involves implicily imposition of boundary lines which must be crossed before a movement is counted as migration. Internal migration refers to the movement which results in a change of usual place of residence within the country. It may consist of the crossing at the village or town boundary, as minimum condition for qualifying the movement as internal migration.[4]

If there is a change in the usual place of residence of a person with reference to his/her birth place, he/she is defined as a migrant according to "Birth-place" concept. If at a time of a population census a change in the usual place of residence is noted with reference to a person's previous usual place of residence the person is termed as a migrant in accordance with the "last residence" concept.[5]

A group of migrants from any one area of origin, resident in a specified area of destination, is referred to as a stream of migrants. For example, migration from rural to urban areas is referred to as a migration stream. The movement in the opposite direction is called its "Counter Stream".[6]

The differentiation of various stream of migration and the determination of both the numbers involved and of the various demographic, social and economic characteristics of migrants is as important as the determination of balance between in and out migration.[7]

There is considerable evidence which indicates that young, educated and unmarried persons have the highest propensity to migrate.[8] Many scholars expect the lowest strata of the rural society to demonstrate the highest propensity to migrate.[9] Agricultural labourers are the reservoir which provides a constant flow of labour into non-agricultural occupations.[10]

If we consider the rural income as the opportunity cost of migration and as a resource for financing of migration expenditure, Banerjee and Kumbar hypothesised that the propensity to migrate is likely to increase with income upto a point and then decrease. This shows that rural development may result in higher migration, not lower. Most of the studies on migration concluded that people migrate, primarily for economic reason. According to Todaro (1969), Harris-Todaro (1970) model, the urban formal sector-wage rates are decided about the market mechanism level, and are downwardly rigid. The reason for this is that excess supply labour. Migrants may not be able to obtain employment in this sector very soon on arrival. They take decision of migration because of either unemployment or very low wages or both in rural area and positive higher difference of rural-urban income. Rural-urban migration so long take place as the expected urban real income exceeds real agricultural income.

Four main stages have been recognised in the development of committed workers. In the first stage uncommitted workers take up industrial employment temporarily and maintain contacts with the villages. The workers go back to their villages after a short period. In the second stage the workers look upon their jobs in industry as permanent but essentially they remain villagers. In the third stage the generally committed workers become completely dependent upon the industries. They minimise their relations with the villages and adjust themselves to the industrial way of life. In the forth stage the workers are attached to particular enterprise and particular occupation.[11]

3. RURAL-URBAN MIGRATION

There are mainly four types of migration namely Rural-Urban migration, Rural-Rural migration, Urban-Urban migration and Urban-Rural migration. These all types of migration are existed in India. But major and main form is rural-urban migration. Therefore, Indian labour migration is basically a rural-urban migration, which is a problem. This is pushed type of migration. Because economic problems pushed labour into urban area from rural area. Most of the study concluded this strong fact of migration.

Poverty and accompanying features is a main reason of Rural-urban migration. This is supported by many studies. Here we can note the major studies, which includes the studies of Michael Mann (1973)[12], Government of India (1956-57)[13], Mahesh Chand (1969)[14], R.C. Saxena (1963)[15], Taxter *et al.* (1956)[16] etc.

Huge unemployment and rare opportunity of employment in rural area is second prime factor for Rural-Urban migration. A significant portion of labour mobility can be explained in terms of lack of alternative opportunities.[17] The supply of land is limited. Most of farm land is depended upon monsoon. Therefore, increasing population put very heavy burden of fixed farm land. This resulted very imbalance between demand and supply of labour which is resulted in the consequently excess supply of labour has to find out employment opportunity elsewhere.[18]

Overburden on cultivated land is one of the important reason for rural-urban migration. Rurals migrate, because they have no sufficient farm land for their subsistence. In this connection ILO study very rightly says, "The small size of agricultural holdings in conjunction with low intensity of production is another factor driving the cultivators for abandon farming.[19]

The process of industrialisation and urbanisation has been mentioned as a crucial factor for rural-urban migration. If we review the literature on Rural-Urban migration two reasons thrown out. Firstly, the big metropolitan commercial and industrial centres are continuously growing centres of employment opportunities. Secondly the industrial competition of these metropolitan areas disloading and closing various village, small-scale and cottage industries, generate and army of unemployed/rural people who are constantly in search of employment.[20]

Some writers have find out in their studies that migration is a source escape for those people who are looked down upon as socially undesirable or degraded owing to their caste position or because of some socially undesirable action on their part.[21] People have forced to leave the places of their origin due to foreign dominance and their exploitations in various ways. This type of school of thought on migration, hold this view are of the opinion that foreign dominance by upsetting the socio-economic balance of an area compel the inhabitants to take shelter in some other place.[22]

Exploitation by local politicians, rulers and landlords is also one of the important reason for rural-urban migration. Panchnan Saha in this connection emphasises that, "There is a strong ground to assume that reason behind migration (in certain cases) was only to seek freedom from a life to incessant toil and shameful exploitation from landlord."[23]

In India, mostly pushed factors are responsible for rural-urban migration. But there are pulled factors which are also responsibles for the same. These includes, better city life, brighter job-wage opportunities, better civil amenities etc.

Some of the studies are thrown on light of joint family for migration. According to these studies, joint family system permits some of the family members to move away for adding to the income of the family, while others can look after family affairs behind.[24]

Rural-urban migration is also connected with age and occupation. Michel mann says that the mobility and particularly long term mobility is significantly co-related to two factors; the occupation and age of the house-hold head. The people in younger age and higher occupational level are more likely to move for manual workers and men over the age of 35 are relatively unlikely to move over long distance.[25]

There is another approach for migration. This can put in the words of Bruce Herrick, who says, "Migration is a function of expected rural-urban income differentials. This, of course, implicitly makes the motivation for migration. Nevertheless, the combination of rural prospects coupled with a more promising urban future is appearing as an explanation of migration."[26]

The pattern of emigration may be classified into the following types:[27]

1. Singleman Emigration.
2. Short-term temporary emigration.
3. Long-term temporary emigration.
4. Permanent emigration.

Ashish Bose[28] raised a question : "Why do people migrate from rural to urban area? Is it because of increasing pressure of population on land and growing unemployment of because of the attractions of city life and better employment opportunities in urban areas? In other words what is the explanation for the continually streams of rural-urban migration? The push of rural misery or the pull of urban living?"

The National Sample Survey Report (No. 53), on internal migration abandons the push and pull approaches and classifies the causes of migration into three categories, namely voluntary, obligatory reasons and sequential reasons.

In an explanatory survey of migration in some villages around Delhi, undertaken by Institute of Economic Growth find out four "Migrant-types" among the underemployed and unemployed population.[29]

1. Those who were not willing to go out of the village at all and wanted employment opportunities within the village.
2. Those who were willing to come to the nearest city from the village, but not to leave the village.
3. Those who were willing to go anywhere if they obtained suitable employment opportunities but wanted their family to stay in the village (This was especially true those who owned lands).
4. Those who were willing to migrate anywhere with their whole families, if suitable employment opportunities were provided to them (This was especially true for landless persons).

The large proportion of the adult male migrants to the cities are married and they live their families behind in the rural areas. The enforced separation from the family persists for long spells in the working life of migrants. In the Delhi Survey, it was found that 71 per cent of migrants were sending money regularly home and of these 90 per cent reported that they had to send money to maintain their families.[30]

According to A.K.Gumber[31] income, social services, differences of opportunities among rural-urban areas, are the main causes of rural-urban migration. People migrate towards more developed areas, from less developed areas. The maximum rate of outmigration was 3.24 in less developed district and the maximum rate of immigration was 8.79 in more developed districts. According to the study, rural-urban migration was 30 per cent in total migration.

4. THEORETICAL ANALYSIS

Many scholars have studies on various aspects of migration and analyse the whole problem. When we analyse theoretically, main important aspect is why labour migrate? Scholars have thrown the light on this crucial issue.

Levis,[32] Fei and Renis,[33] stated that differences of employment and wages among rural-urban areas is a main reason for migration. If the marginal productivity of these migrant people is zero in original employment sectors, the migration will increase in the productivity. It is assumed that this employment differences would disappear in future. According to this model migration from one place to another will continue upto wage-equalisation of these two places. The main assumptions of this model are migrants interested in increasing in income, perfect knowledge about employment market, they possess skill and interest, there are no social obstacles on ways of migration and capital market is perfect.[34] This is somewhat traditional model presented by traditional economists.

Decision of migration is very important in whole migration process. This decision is taking with the context of migration incentives. Decision making analysis of migration very clearly indicates that migrants moves towards region of brighter economic opportunities from region of lesser employment opportunities. This is true for both developing and developed countries.

The studies of Lowry[35], Beals[36], Sahota[37], Greenwood[38] also supported this approach. Before this Revenstein[39] also analysed the same. These all studies show the relation between migration flows and economic opportunities.

Lee[40] had represented the theory of Revenstein in the form of general theory. He analysed the factors affecting on migration. He classified these factors into four parts, namely, factors connected with origin region, factors affecting migration region, obstacles factors and individual factors.

Well established generalisation is that pushed factors are more important than pulled factors in underdeveloped countries. Studies of Asian countries repeatedly supported this generalisatlon. Hanser[41] stated that migrants pushed to cities from villages. This will create unemployment, economic and social problems in Asian cities. This will transform rural poverty into urban poverty.

Macro analysis of migration is not able to draw a clear cut picture of migration. There are many drawbacks in macro-level migration analysis. As the circumstances, problems, prospects are changed, the macro-analysis is not able to explain about migration. In this context macro type of analysis of migration is very useful and important for truly understand the whole concept.

Analysis on migration presented by Rempel[42], Calwell[43], Sabot[44], etc. have concluded migration differences in detail. These deriving conclusions are due to application of micro-level analysis. These are the studies of countries of Asia, Africa and Latin America. There migrants were age of 15-29 of years. One of the main conclusion of the study, mostly youth migrate because they are benefited life-time.

Becker[45] concluded that very long earning time period, and early entry in the job are the main factors of migration for youth. Schultz[46] find out that an importance of rural-urban wage difference has decreased as increasing of age.

Connel, *et al.*, concluded the same.[47] But Hanser[48] disagrees with the statement that migrants are rural poors and unemployers. Actually very small part of rural poors migrate. It is true that rural economic situation is weak but it is not sufficient, proper and perfect for complete migration.

According to study of Huntigton migrants give Topmost priority to place at where relatives and friends are there.[49]

This theoretical analysis of migration throws the light on why, how, where, people migrate.

5. EVILS EFFECTS OF MIGRATION

Migration is a problem of labour sector. It is not only a labour problem, but it leads the problem of urbanisation, urban poverty and unemployment, slums and pollution problems and many other institutional, social, cultural, educational problems. Migration disturb the whole family and social life of labourers. The life of labourers become wandering here and there under the shadows of uncertainty of employment and wages. He becomes a victim of unstable and insecure pitiable poor life.

Ram Avtar[50] narrated that instead of fresh meals cooked by their wives and ready for them in their huts or brought to their fields, they have to subsist on stale, course and dirty meals, which are cooked by strangers and for which heavy charges have to be paid. Such food tempts them to go small and cheap restaurant and liquor-shops, where the food served is spicier but less nourishing and where the habit of drinking is begun or strengthened. Most of the study on migration concluded about single migration. Migrant has to leave his wife behind him in the village. He is not able to be happier and healthy rural and family life. Migrant lives alone in the city where he becomes victim of prostitution, gambling and alcoholism. This leads heavy reduction in efficiency, productivity and competitiveness of labourers.

Migration is important cause for problems of urbanisation, *i.e.* problems of Housing, Health, Sanitation, Institutional, Social and related problems. The housing of the migrants combined the worst characteristics of both the rural and urban slums. Not only were the sites most insanitary but the material used for creating huts was also very filthy. Forsaken places like the sloped along the railway lines, banks of open drainage streams, waste land adjoining the dirty localities in the towns, open spaces earmarked for dumping the town refuse etc. which no one else would think of utilising were chosen by them.[51]

Migration badly affected on efficiency and productivity of workers and whole industrial mechanism. National Commission on labour has observed, "In the past turnover of labour and casual work were not merely a result of lack of commitment on the part of the workers, but also of employers reluctance to bear the burden implied in hiring permanent labour. As industry expanded to include a wide variety of skilled and unskilled jobs, industrial work ceased to be the monopoly of migrants from villages."

INTUC pointed out, "We consider that the only way of securing a stabilised labour force and for the protection of the interests of the industrial workers, firstly to provide adequate housing accommodation for them in the industrial centres, and secondly to make provision for their maintenance during illness, unemployment and old age."

6. CONCLUSION

This all analysis or narration shows that migration is very serious, dangerous and destructive problem. Government's false Planning, Policies, Priorities, Strategies of development is responsible for this dangerous problem. Government give topmost importance and priority to industry instead of agriculture, to urbanisation instead of rural development, to giant mega industries instead of small scale, cottage and agro-based industries. The result of these is faster migration which is a root of many problems. If this process of migration will remain continue, very giant problems would arise which would destruct the whole economy, society and democratic political system.

The time has come for rethinking about this crucial problem of migration. We should change our priorities, strategies and whole policies. We should give topmost priority to agriculture and allied sectors, rural development, cottage, small-scale and agro-based industries, and industrial and economic decentralisation. We should develop tiny village industries, artisaning, dairying and animal husbandry, forestry in rural industries. Unemployment, Poverty elimination programmes should be converted into self-employment programmes. If this would become possible, each and every country-men or member of the labour force would obtain gainful productive employment at their native place. The rate of migration would automatically decrease.

REFERENCES

1. Thomas, Barinely (1973), *Migration and Economic Development*, Cambridge University Press, p. 26.
2. Singh, Mohinder (1976), *Socio-Economic Problems of Migrant Labour of Kashmir*, Ph.D. thesis, University of Jammu, ch. 1, p. 1.
3. United Nations Organisation (1970), *Methods of Measuring Internal Migration*, Manual VI, New York.
4. Soni, N.K. (1985), "Dimensions of Migration in India", *The Indian Journal of Labour Economics*, Vol. XXVIII, No. 3, October, pp. 146-170.
5. *Ibid.*
6. Kothari, Devendra and Pravin Visaria (1985), "Rural-urban Migration and its Counter-stream in Gujarat : A Study of Census Data", *The Indian Journal of Labour Economics*, Vol. XVIII, No. 1 and 2, April-July, pp. 77-94.
7. Thomas, D.S. (1938), "Research Memorandum on Migration Differentials", *Social Science Research Council*, Bull. No. 43, New York.
8. Banerjee, Biswjit (1986). "Who Migrates and Why?", in (ed.), *Rural to Urban Migration and the Urban Labour Market : A Case Study of Delhi*, K. Krishna Murthy, Himalaya Publishing House, Delhi. p. 3.
9. Myrdal, Gunnar (1968), Asian Drama, *An Enquiry into the Poverty of Nations*, Peuguin Book Ltd., Hardmondsworth, p. 471.
10. International Labour Organisation (1960), *Why Labour Leaves the Land*, Geneva, p. 125.
11. Ram Avtar (1971), *Lectures on Labour Problems and Social Welfare in India*, New Academic Publishing Company, Jullunder, p. 1.
12. Mann, Michael, (1937), *Workers of Move : Sociology of Reallocation*, Cambridge University Press, p. 80.
13. Government of India (1956-57), *Report of the Second Agriculture Labour Enquiry*, Labour Bureau, p. 94.

14. Chand, Mahesh (1969), *Employment and Migration in Allahabad City*, Oxford and Ich Publishing Company, Calcutta, p. 108.
15. Saxena, R.C. (1963), *Labour Problems and Social Welfare*, Jai Prakash Nath, Meerut, p. 19.
16. Texter, Hussain and Deshmukh (1956), *Social Implications of Industrialisation and Urbanisation*, Research Centre on the Social Implications of Industrialisation in South Asia, Calcutta, p. 53.
17. U.S. Department of Labour (1960), "Labour Supply in a Newly Industrialised Area", *Bulletin* No. 1261, February, p. 22.
18. Bhogoliwal, T.N. (1956), *Labour Problems in India*, Kitabghar, Kanpur, p. 8.
19. I.L.O. (1960), *op. cit.*, p. 127.
20.
(A) Donald, J. Bouges (1969), "Internal Migration", in Hansar and Dancan (ed.), *The Study of Population*, The University of Chicago Press, Chicago, p. 487.
(B) Robert, L. Stein (1969), "Unemployment and Job-Mobility", *Monthly Labour Review*, U.S. Department of Labour, April, p. 337.
(C) I.L.O. (1960), *op. cit.*, p. 128.
(D) Bhogoliwal, T.N. (1956), *op. cit.*, p. 180.
(E) Saxena, R.C. (1963), *op. cit.*, p. 19.
21.
(A) Charles, Myers (1959), *Labour Problem in Industrialisation in India*, pp. 38-39.
(B) IORC (1977), *Social Change and Internal Migration : A Review of Research Findings from Africa, Asia and Latin America*, Ottawa, p. 82.
22.
(A) Michael Todaro (1976), *op. cit.*, p. 16.
(B) Panchanan Saha (1970), *op. cit.*, p. 46.
23.
(A) T. Paul Shultz (1971), *Rural-Urban Migration in Cambodia.*
(B) Prabhu Hussain and Deshmukh (1958), *op. cit.*, p. 56.
24. Saxena, R.C. (1963), *op. cit.*, p. 19.
25. Michael Mann, (1973), *op. cit.*, p. 9.
26. Bruce, H. Herrick (1965), *Urban Migration and Economic Development : A Published Ph. D. Thesis*, M.I.T. Press, Cambridge, London, p. 12.
27. Saxena, D.P. (1977), *Rural-Urban Migration in India*, Popular Prakashana, Mumbai.
28. Bose Ashish (1965), "Why do people migrate the cities?", *Yojana*, Vol. IX, No. 1, January, 22, pp. 25-26, and 32.
29. Maheta, Dinesh, B. (1981), *Behavioural Aspects of Rural-Urban Migration*, School of Planning, Centre for Environmental Planning and Technology, Ahmedabad.
30. Rao, V.K.R.V. (1963), *The City of Greater Delhi*, Institute of Economic Growth, Delhi.
31. Gumber, A.K. (1983), Sectoral Level of Development and Migration in Gujarat : A District Level Analysis", *Anvesak*, Vol. XIII, No. 1, June, pp. 25-46.
32. Lewis, A.W. (1964), *Development with Unlimited Supply of Labour*, Manchester School of Economic and Social Studies, March, Manchester.
33. Fei., G. and Ranis (1972), "Critique of Probabilities Model : Application of some Markov Models of Migration", *Journal of Mathematical Sociology*, pp. 233-282.

34. Fabricant, F.A. (1970), "An Expectational Model of Migration", *Journal of Regional Science*, 10, pp. 13-25.
35. Lowry, I.S. (1966), *Migration and Metropolitan Growth : Two Analytical Models*, San Fransisco.
36. Beals, R.E. *et al.* (1969), "Rationality and migration in Ghana", *Review of Economics and Statistics*, 49, p. 480-86.
37. Sahota, G.S. (1968), "An Economic Analysis of Intemal Migration of Brazil", *Journal of Political Economy*, Vol. 76 (2).
38. Greenwood, M. (1971), "An Analysis of the Determinant of Labour Mobility in India", *Annals of Regional Science*, 5 (1).
39. Revenstein, E.G. (1985), "The Laws of Migration", *Journal of the Statistical Society*, 48, June, p. 167-227.
40. Lee, Everett (1967), *A Theory of Migration*, Demography, 3, p. 47-57.
41. Hanser, P.M. (1957), *Urbanisation in Asia and for East, UNESCO*, Research Centre on the Social Implications of Urbanisation of Southern Asia, Calcutta.
42. Rempel, H. (1970), *Labour Migration into Urban Centres and Urban Unemployment in Kenya*, Unpublished Ph.D. Thesis, University of Wisconsin.
43. Caldwell, J. (1969), *African Rural-Urban Migration : The Movement to Ghana's Towns*, Hurst, London.
44. Sabot, R.H. (1972), *Education, Income Distribution and Urban Migration in Tanzania*, University of Dares Salaam, Mimeo.
45. Becker, G.S. (1964), *Human Capital*, N.B.E.R., New York.
46. Schultz, T.P. (1971), "Rural-Urban Migration in Columbia", *Review of Economics and Statistics*, Vol. 53(2).
47. Connel, *et al.* (1976), *Migration from Rural Areas : The Evidence from Village Studies*, Oxford University Press, New Delhi, for the I.L.O.
48. Hanser, *Ibid.*
49. Hantigton (1974), *An Empirical Study of Ethnic Linkages in Kenya*, Rural-Urban Migration, Unpublished Ph.D. Thesis, SUBY, Binghampton.
50. Ram Avtar; *op. cit.*, p. 3.
51. *Ibid.*

7

Absentism and Labour Turnover

"At the time of work, if work is not attended it is called Absentism."

— *K.G. Fenelan*

Outline of the Chapter

1. Absentism :
   (A) Meaning and definition of Absentism.
   (B) Rate of Absentism.
   (C) Absentism of industrial labour in India.
   (D) Main causes of Absentism.
   (E) Effects of Absentism.
   (F) Remedies to reduce labour Absentism.
2. Labour turnover
   (A) Meaning and definition.
   (B) Rate of labour turnover.
   (C) Labour turnover in India.
   (D) Causes of labour turnover in India.
   (E) Disadvantages of labour turnover.
   (F) Remedies to reduce labour turnover.

1. ABSENTISM

There are several problems in Indian labour. Absentism and labour turnover are two main problems among them. As they are from rural areas, continuity of their relations with rural area and due to certain other reasons the rate of absentism is much high among them. Similarly sizable labour turnover are there. They frequently change their industry, business or profession. These both problems adversely effects not only to labour or industry but also to the whole economy. So, it becomes necessary to study both these problems. First of all, let us study meaning and definition of absentism to know the problem of absentism.

(A) Meaning and definition of Absentism

Generally, Absentism means to remain absent without informing (prior permission). But in industry "Absentism" has specific meaning. Some experts have defined "Absentism". Some of them are as under :

1. *Dr. J.D. Haikat.* Absentism means unsteady disturbance (interruption) in work. Its minimum duration must be one day. The maximum expectation of the labour on the day that he will go for his work and if he doesn't go for work is also called as Absentism.

2. *Prof. Ankalikar.* Not to attend one's work improperly or in unauthorised manner is called absentism.

3. *K.G. Fenelan.* Not to attend the duty during duty hours is called Absentism.

4. *Labour Department.* Rate of absentism is that percentage of work where work has not performed.

From the above definitions it is clear that during working days, if without prior permission and showing improper reason, a labour does not attend the work is called "absentism". In such condition a labourer remains absent, though he is fit for his duty, This absentism is unauthorised and voluntary. Specific reason for the absentism is not being mentioned by the labourer. General leaves are not included in absentism. Absentism is such a situation that which can be controlled or prevented.

(B) Rate of Absentism

Different methods are adopted to know the volume of absentism in different industries. To know the rate of absentism in different units at different places, different situations are taken into account; hence, specific method is not developed. Here it must be clear that mere absence of worker cannot be called absentism. There are three possibilities for that; he may come late or remain absent or leave the job. So in this context it is difficult to measure absentism precisely. Due to this reason "Indian Royal Commission on Labour" has narrated in its report that absentism is a complex phenomena, which includes possible absentism due to many reasons. So there are some employers who can judge which labour has not resumed the duty, who is sick, who is on leave or who is on tour. Hence, the labour who has not gone with a view to leave the job is considered as absent.

The rate of absentism can be known by dividing human hour loss by total human working hour. Thus, it is essential to know two main factors for determining the rate of absentism. To know human loss hours it is essential to know about number of absent labourers, shifts and working hours. The another factor is total working hours and total shifts during which work is being done. With the help of these details we can know rate of absentism by dividing total human hour loss by total human working hours.

Some precautions should be taken while determining the rate of absentism; such as the labourer cannot be called absent, if he remains present for very short period. Strike or lock out can't be considered as absentism. If a labourer leaves the job without intimation, he may be considered as absent; till his name is continued in muster roll. The labourer who is on leave with prior consent of the departmental head, he can't be called absent. Worker can be considered as absent, if he is aware of his duty hours and remains absent, when he is not anticipated to remain absent. Thus, volume of absentism should be counted, considering all these factors.

(C) Absentism of Industrial Labour in India

The rate of absentism in Indian Industrial labour is much higher compared to other nations of the world. In India there is no specific system to know Industrial absentism figure. The labour bureau published statistics of industrial absentism of certain industries of specific centres. Except that no authentic information is available, if we analyse the figures provided by Indian labour year book, labour gazettes and other publications, we can say that absentism in coal mines is 13 per cent, in gold mine (Mysore) 15.5 per cent, textile industries (Mumbai) 19 per cent, Ahmedabad 15 per cent, Madurai 16.3 per cent, Kanpur 16.7 per cent, in engineering industry it was 16.7 per cent in Mumbai, 16.7 per cent in Bengal and it was 17.2 per cent in Mysore.

In 1987 the rate of absentism was 18.1 per cent in textile industries, in Iron and Steel industries 15.6 per cent, 12.2 per cent in Cement industries, 23.1 per cent in Match box industries and 17.7 per cent in Telegraph Workshop.[1] Compared to 1971 (volume) amount of absentism was increased in Iron and Steel industries, Match box and Telegraph Work industries; while it decreased in Textile and Cement industries.

(D) Main Causes of Absentism

It is clear from these figures that the rate of absentism in industrial labours of India is much high. There are some specific reasons for that which varies according to different places and industries. Yet, there are some common causes as under :

1. Attachment with native. Most of the Indian Industrial workers come from rural area. They have great feelings and attachment to their native. So, they frequently visit there to meet their relatives and friends. Due to this reason large amount of absentism is observed in industries.

According to a survey conducted in Mumbai 47 per cent workers visit their native once in a year, 38 per cent twice a year and 6 per cent thrice a year.

2. Excess workload. People coming from rural area who work as industrial workers have to work in congested and unnatural atmosphere. They can't adjust themselves in such condition continuously till a very long time. They have to work at a specific place, in this work they do not have any interest or zeal. So, they feel their duty very hard and burdensome. As they get tired or become sick, return to their native. Amount of absentism increases due to these frequent reasons. Prof. Williams says that as the workers have to work in unknown industries, they cannot adjust themselves in such work; that is the main cause of absentism. Amount of absentism is higher in the workers who are not acquainted with industrial discipline.

3. Poor health and sickness. Sickness is a major cause of absentism in industrial workers. They do not get nutritive food in city. So, they easily become the victim or diseases like malaria, typhoid, diarrhoea, vomiting and stomach diseases. They also become victim of fatigue.

Absentism due to illness is 4 per cent in India, 1.1 per cent in Canada, 2.6 per cent in Italy, 1.9 per cent in America and 3.2 per cent in Belgium.

4. Problem of residence. The workers get employment in cities but they can't accommodate their family in city. Because, the house rent is so high that they can't afford it. So, their family stay at native and they have to frequently visit their native. Due to this reason they can't work regularly and hence, amount of absentism increases.

5. Bad habits and addicts. The labourer whose family is in native lives lonely and they become victim of bad habits like gambling, drinking etc. They also become drug addicted. Due to these reasons they are unable to work regularly.

6. Accidents and mishaps. There is no sufficient facility to work safely in Indian factories. Machineries are very old too. In small place so many workers work together. Due to all these reasons accidents or mishaps take place often. Hence, injured worker cannot work regularly. So, he remains absent for long time.

In 1951 rate of injured workers due to accidents or mishaps was

2993 per lakh workers in factories while in mines it was 547. Whereas in 1986 this rate was 4961 in factories and in mines 241.[2]

Number of compensated injuries were as under :

In 1951 — 63133
1961 — 93737
1971 — 57346
1981 — 34446 and
in 1985 — 20499.

7. Natural climate. Workers coming from rural areas do not suit city atmosphere and climate. During three months *i.e.* from April to June days are very hot. In these hot days workers have to work in the factories, which become unbearable. So during these days for protection from hot and terrible atmosphere he goes to his native.

8. Social cause. Indian workers are highly impressed by social traditions. He has to attend social functions at native. He has to visit native often to attain their family and social responsibilities. So, in industries rate of absentism is very high.

9. Religious causes. Indian labourers are highly impressed by religious beliefs too. So, during religious occasions they have to visit their native. They have to visit their native during celebration of religious festivals or religious occasions. So, he can't perform his duty regularly.

10. Debt. Due to poverty Indian workers become debtor. They take loans or borrow money from moneylenders or merchant. He can't return this debt in time. He feels that creditors/moneylenders will come to collect their money at his work's place and so, he does not attend the work. Due to this also volume of absentism remains high.

11. Misbehaviour of employer or supervisor. An employer or a supervisor who looks after his work behaves with him improperly. He tortures workers differently or he exploits variously. Due to their behaviour he gets tired. Hence, sometimes worker remains absent for long time.

12. Fatigue and boredom. Without any interest he works continuously in a totally new atmosphere. So, he finds his work tiresome and boring. Their work become painful and unbearable. So, rest becomes inevitable for them. That is why he can't attend his duty regularly.

13. Mental imbalance. Though this factor has been neglected, it has got direct connection with workers absentism. Durganand Sinha has mentioned in his study that most of the workers who remain absent are being suffered by mental imbalance. This imbalance may be by birth.

Such persons can't maintain their performance in duty as well as they can't maintain their family. This is also a factor of absentism.

14. Family disputes. Workers have to visit their native often due to frequent family disputes. This is also a major cause for workers absentism.

15. Duty and nightshift. The workers have to work according to shift system. They have to work also in the night shift for which they are not habituated. So, they cannot work at that time. Hence, they have to remain absent.

16. Problems of transportation. Generally, working place is very far from the residential areas. Workers do not have their personal vehicles. So, they have to go by public transport facility. Due to irregular transportation they reach late very often. Thus, even though they are willing they can't go for work.

Besides that they can't go on duty punctually, due to reasons like admission of children, court cases and such other reasons. In this Way in India industrial worker remain absent due to various reasons. Thus, factors like work related factor, native related social factors and religious factors are responsible for absentism. Workers cannot come on duty due to these factors.

(E) Effects of Absentism

Due to labour absentism some specific effect is being created. Regarding this, Labour Commission said that due to absentism both parties suffer. It adversely effects labourer's income. On other side production also has adverse effect due to labourers irregularity and indiscipline. Labourers absentism reduce their income. It effects their standard of living. Their living standard is low and hence, health deteriorates. In addition deteriorated income adversely effects all these factors. Not only this but it also creates adverse effects on their employment. According to Shri V.V. Giri, "Continuous and causelers absentism leads to loss of employment." Absentism also effects adversely to the labour union activities.

On another side producer also suffers loss due to labour absentism. It directly effects production. Labour absentism reduces production. Excess absentism of workers badly effect production system and working method. Due discipline cannot be maintained and clashes between workers and employer increases.

(F) Remedies to Reduce Labour Absentism

Labour absentism is a problem in industries. It also highlights drawbacks of Economy and Social structure. Shri T.L.A. Acharya says, that labour absentism in industry indicates that various types of evils have entered into the society.[3] Therefore, efforts must be taken to remove the grave problem of absentism. This problem is more social than economic. Some important suggestions to solve this problem are as under :

1. Rate of absentism can be reduced by labour welfare measures. They can be made hale and happy by providing them facilities like sports and games, picnic, entertainment etc. Thus, they will not feel fatigue or boredom and heavy work also.
2. They should be provided furnished residential facility. If he could keep his family with him, then his frequent native visit due to this reason would be curtailed.
3. Working environment must be improved. Working condition should be such that labourer do not feel fatigue or boredon during their work. There should be sufficient light, cleanliness, moisture etc. where labourer works.
4. Labourers should be given (adequate) wages which will increase their income as well as willingness to work. Hence, absentism will decrease.
5. Sufficient leave must be granted. So, they can take adequate (sufficient) rest.
6. Adequate steps should be taken to provide them protection against accidents and illness.
7. They should be explained in detail for not to remain absent and they should be explained benefits due to their presence and drawbacks due to absentism.
8. Steps should be taken to protect them from misbehaviour by employer, supervisor or officers.

If above mentioned steps are taken, labour absentism can be reduced. Mainly financial and working encouragement, as well as all possible facilities should be provided, so that willingness to work increases. All these steps can reduce labour absentism. Hence, labourers, owners, industry and the whole economy could be saved from loss due to absentism.

2. LABOUR TURNOVER

(A) Meaning and Definition

During certain period in some industry change of staff or transfer of labour is called as labour turnover. In other words, if old or routine staff left the industry, firm or factory and appointment of new staff is called as change or turnover.

Labour investigation committee defines labour turnover or change as, "rate of changes in number of labourers during certain period in any mill can be defined". In other words labour turnover shows exit of old labourers and entry of new labourers in any industry.

In any factory rate of labourers who have left the factory and the new labourers appointed at their place is called as rate of labour turnover. For *e.g.*, suppose, in a factory during certain period out of 100 labourers, 5 labourers left the factory and if 5 labourers have to be appointed at their place, then rate of labour turnover would be 5 per cent.

There is clear difference between labour turnover or change of labour and absentism. In labour absentism he does not attend the work, but never leaves. He resumes his work (duty) again. In labour change or turnover old workers leave the work (job) and new workers take their place. In this way labour turnover highlights (shows) two things. *viz.*, (1) old workers give up the work and (2) new workers accept the work.

(B) Rate of Labour Turnover

In India no specific method is developed to measure labour change or turnover. So, reliable figures are not available, although there are some formulas for measurement. According to one formula, if number of left workers during certain period in any industry is divided by total number of workers, we get rate of labour change.

To measure labour turnover, U.S.A.'s labour statistical department gives following formula :

$$L.T. = A + S \div \frac{P_1 + P_2}{2} \times \frac{365}{M}$$

Where,

(1) L.T. = Labour turnover

(2) A = Addition of labour

(3) S = Decrease of labour

(4) P_1 = Number of labourers in the beginning of the month.

(5) P_2 = Number of labourers at the end of the month.

(6) M = Number of absentism days during the month.

This American formula can be explained as under :

1. Addition of increase or decrease in number of labourers.
2. Add the number of workers in the beginning of the month.
3. Divide first (No. 1) numbers' figures by second (No. 2) numbers' figures.
4. Divide 365 by month's average absentism.
5. Multiply number 3 and number 4's figures.

By above calculations we can know rate of labour turnover or turnover.

Although there are some difficulties in calculation of labour turnover, no specific records have been maintained regarding workers who had left and entry of new workers. Similarly during boom and dull situation also there is vast increase or decrease in number of workers. During measurement of labour turnover difference between absentism and labour turnover can't be maintained. Due to all these reasons we can't measure labour turnover or turnover properly.

(C) Labour Turnover in India

According Royal Commission for Labour, in most of the factories 5 per cent new appointments of staff are there per month. Labour Inquiry Commission have mentioned rate of labour turnover in some industries. According to that rate of labour turnover in cotton textile industry 0.6 per cent, in woollen textile industry 0.4 per cent, in gold mines 1.6 per cent, in glass industry 1.2 per cent and in rice factories were 3.1 per cent.

In engineering industry rate of labour turnover was 3.1 per cent, in Tamilnadu 3.1 per cent and in West Bengal it was 1.6 per cent. In Maharashtra rate of labour turnover was less where number of labourers in factory was more than 2000. But in Gujarat rate of labour turnover was very less in the factories where number of labourers were between 501 to 1000. There is labour turnover almost in each Indian industry but this rate is higher in unorganised sector industry. Where the proportion of casual or temporary labourers is more than permanent labourers there labour turnover or turnover rate is higher. But labour turnover rate is low where proportion of permanent labourer is more (higher).

(D) Causes of Labour Turnover in India

Some specific factors are responsible for labour turnover. According to Labour Inquiry Commission resignation given by them is mainly responsible for labour turnover. Also (although) labourers are being relieved from the job, but its proportion is very low. Labour turnover or turnover depends on the factors like place, time, situation, type (nature) of profession, owner's nature, nature of working unit, working method etc. Some main reasons for labour turnover are as under :

1. Natural causes. One important reason for labour turnover is natural factors. Due to these reasons labourer has to give up the work compulsorily. The factors effecting their fitness for work are long illness, their death, old age, accident, serious injury etc. Due to all these natural causes he has to give up the work.

2. Resignation given by workers. Problem of labour turnover arises when any worker gives his resignation to employer of the factory where he works. Due to reasons like serious illness, accident, getting opportunity elsewhere, foreign trip, unable to work etc. he resigns from his current job then new staff is being recruited. In this way labour turnover problem arises. Mainly due to resignation of the staff (employee) only this problem arises.

3. Dismissal from service. Sometimes labourer is being dismissed or removed from the service by their owner or employer. Labourers are being dismissed due to the reasons like indiscipline, misbehaviour, involvement in scandal, damage to factory, active participation in strike, dull market, closing of any department, mechanisation, continuous dissatisfaction in work etc. Naturally, this time it effects number of labourers.

4. Transfer system. It there is transfer system in the factory then also labour turnover takes place. In transfer system to adjust employees coming from another sections routine employees are being shifted to elsewhere. In this way labour turnover takes place.

5. End of specific work. There are same specific work or works in some factories. After completion of specialised work that worker is being relieved. Again, when this work is being started, at that time they are re-employed

6. High rate of excess labour. In India supply of labour is more than its demand and so supply of excess labour is more. These labourers are ready to work at very low rate. Hence, owner or employer relieves old labourers and employes new labourers at cheap rate.

7. Seasonal work. Some professions or industries are of seasonal type. In these professions or industries more workers are employed in season and when season is over excess labourers are relieved. In this way during seasonal and unseasonal time labour turnover continues.

8. Project type work. In this type of work project work is to be done at different places and at different time. This project may be of different type and size. Here when new project starts employees are employed and when project is over, employees get relieved. Again, when project starts employees and workers are going employed. In this way labour turnover continues.

9. Probability of being promoted elsewhere. When worker finds that he will not get progress in the same unit, but if he joins another unit, will get chance of progress. Hence, he leaves the routine unit and will join another unit.

10. Low wage and exploitation. When worker finds that he gets low wage where he works and also severally he is being exploited, at that time he will leave the unit and will join another unit.

11. Attachment with native. Workers come to the city for employment from their native. But as he is deeply attached with native; he can't settle in the city. Hence, at last he leaves the job and returns to native.

12. Due to residence problem also he returns to his native.

13. When the work is hard and unbearable, then also he can't works, at that time leaves the work.

14. Due to international reunity, economical and political changes there is large scale industrial labour turnover.

15. When there is vast changes in government's industrial policy, then also large scale labour turnover takes place.

16. When worker does not get leave and his native visit is unavoidable, if this problem continues then also he leaves his recent employment and tries to settle at comparatively good place.

17. When worker does not adjust himself in new atmosphere due to difference in caste, religion and language then also he leaves recent profession.

In this way different factors are responsible for labour turnover or turnover. Due to all these factors old workers leave the industry and new workers employment become necessary.

(E) Disadvantage of Labour Turnover

Labour Inquiry Commission had informed that labour turnover is such impediment that we can't use human and physical resources. Labourers, owners or employers, industries and economy each has suffer loss due to labour turnover. Continuous instability take place in labourers employment and their work. They can't get permanent workers' benefits. Similarly, he could not get cash and kind benefits of continuous profession. Also, he does not get seniority benefits. Often and continuous change in profession effects adversely to his working ability, continuity and specialisation. Labourer has to spend much to find new work. Change of work also increases his burden of work. Labour turnover also effects adversely to labour unions.

Labour turnover also effects owners improperly and adversely. Labour turnover directly effect production and productivity. Owner has to bear the expense of working information or education or training to new workers. In starting new workers have low productivity. Unit does not get benefits of old workers. Labour turnover affected the use of machineries and equipments.

Where there is more labour turnover in industry, there it adversely effects its productivity. If we consider the whole economy then also labour turnover effects production, employment, income etc. It also effects development of the area.

(F) Remedies to Reduce Labour Turnover

Above matter indicates that the problem of labour turnover is not limited upto any unit only but to some extent it is an industrial, economical and social problem. So, it becomes necessary to take steps to solve this problem. The problem of labour turnover can be minimised by investigating causes of the problem and steps to solve the problem. Recommendations for these are as under :

1. Labour recruitment type, procedure and time should be changed. There should be some special administration for the same. This recruitment should be procedural system of recruitment at random and retrenchment should be ended.
2. Worker should be given sufficient wage. He should not be exploited by any means.
3. Financially they should be protected by social security schemes.
4. They should be provided adequate residential facility so that they may not run away to the native due to this reason.
5. There should be sufficient facilities where he works. He should be given such facilities that he does not find any strain during the work.
6. Labour should get benefits of promotion and other allowances and incentives.
7. Various steps should be taken for labour welfare.
8. Human and intimate treatment should be given to the labourers by owner or employers or supervisors or officers and heads.
9. Steps should be taken considering improvement in labourers' economic condition and his standard of living.
10. Labour should get benefits of Bonus, Pension, Provident Fund, Gratuity etc.
11. Working hours should be reduced. Working procedure, system and condition should be easy and good.
12. The labour union should be more sound and effective, so that problems of workers can be solved and they may not change their profession frequently.
13. Procedure of making labourer permanent should be speedy, system should be arranged to prevent the under-retrenchment.

Labour turnover can be reduced by these steps. They shall not leave the unit, if they will be given enough wage, facilities, benefits, incentives and task simplified. They also do not like uncertainty and instability, but some intolerable factors force them to leave the unit.

The problem of labour absentism and turnover is serious, not only for industries but also for whole economy. There is difference between absentism and turnover. Basically, both are different problems though there are some similarity between them. These problems create grave effect.

They adversely effect worker, employer, industry and economy. In underdeveloped nations this problem is much and more serious compared to developed nations. These are in India too. In some industries this problem is very much and very serious. Steps have been taken at industrial and government level. Still these problems exist today also.

REFERENCES

1. Pocket Book of Labour Statistics, 1987-1989.
2. Indian Labour Statistics, 1979 and Pocket Book of Labour Statistics, 1987.
3. Acharya, T.L.A., *Planning for Labour*.

8

Trade Unionism

"A union is a continuous association of persons in industry — whether employees or independent workers — formed primarily for the purpose of the pursuit of the interest of its members of the trade they represent."

— *S.D. Punekar*

Outline of the Chapter

1. Introduction.
2. Definitions of Trade Unionism.
3. Characteristics of Trade Unions.
4. Trade Unions and their functions in other countries.
5. Functions of Trade Unions in India.
6. International Observation on the Role of Trade Union.
7. Principles Regulating Functions of Trade Union.

1. INTRODUCTION

Tendency of unity increased among workers as industries developed and more and more people started working in industrial units. They were being exploited and labour problems increased. Labourers were inspired to be united due to insecurity and problems of existence. Karl Marx appealed labourers for being united, remove capitalism and to handle industries. Thus, in various nations labour unions were formed and developed. A specific thinking came in existence for solving labour problems and labour functions. This is known as Trade Unionism.

2. DEFINITIONS OF TRADE UNIONISM

It is very difficult to define Trade Unionism, as it has got various angles and functions. Its form and function varies according to nation and area. Yet, various trade unions, authors, units and organisation have defined it according to various aspects. Some defined it as union of employee or industrial workers. Some includes other unions too in it. But most of them accepts that purpose of trade union is to protect benefits of their members, solve their problems and overall welfare.

Some important definitions of Trade Union are as under :

1. "A union is a continuing, long term association of employees, formed and maintained for the specific purpose of advancing and protecting the interest of members in their working relationship."

   — *Dale*

2. "A union is a continuous association of persons in industry — whether employees or independent workers formed primarily for the purpose of the pursuit of the interest of its members of the trade they represent."

   — *S.D. Punekar*

3. "Trade Union is a continuous long-term organisation of employees. Its purpose is to maintain current living condition and improvement in it."

   — *Sydney Webb*

4. "Trade Union is a monopolised complex of wage earning people, who are supplementary to each other as personal producer. But they depend on employer for selling their labour. Its main purpose is to increase bargaining power with employer or collective bargaining.".

   — *J. Cunison*

5. "A Trade Union means an association of workers in one or more professions an association carried on mainly for the purpose of protecting and advancing the member's economic interest."

   — *G.D.H. Cole*

6. "It's a continuous voluntary organisation of the people who get wage, salary and fee which :

   (1) protects and improve their life style;

   (2) controls relation of both side with state government through mutual discussion;

   (3) it makes wage and salary earners partner at national stage as a collective producer group.

   — *N. Barou*

7. "It is a Union of Producers in which people get united to get compensation in state units, co-operative units, private units and professions. Union negotiates with various state agencies for their

members. It represents in all meetings of labour and social welfare and thus, comes on conclusion of accord and consent"

— *Soviet Labour Code,* Article *151*

8. "Union or organisation means an amalgamation whose main purpose is to regulate relation between worker and employer, employer and employer, worker and worker; to set up ethics for any trade or profession and to make provision for welfare of their members."

—*British Trade Union Act,* 1958

9. "Trade union is a large organisation of the class of workers whose wage is their total or main source of income, who do physical or mental work, who get ad hoc employment in industrial units, institutes and schools."

— *According to Trade Union Act of China*

10. "Trade Union is a permanent or temporary amalgamation whose main aim is to restrict relations between labourers and owners, owners and owners, labourers and labourers."

— *According to Trade Union Act, 1926 of India*

11. "Trade Unions are essentially associations of manual and/or non-manual work. People, including professional grades, formed to safeguard and improve the working conditions of their members and more generally to raise their status and promote their vocational interest."

— *Richardson*

12. "It is an organisation, incorporated or otherwise, consisting of employees. The organisation on acts in the collective interests of the employees in negotiating with employers, particularly in matters of wages and working conditions."

— *Sloan and Zurcher*

13. "It is an association of workers in a particular trade or a craft organised to promote a common interest and to further that interest through negotiation of wages, hours and other conditions of employment."

— *Rovert's Dictionary of Industrial Relations*

3. CHARACTERISTICS OF TRADE UNIONS

Above definitions give us information regarding trade union, its functions and aims. Its main characteristics are as under :

1. Trade Union is a continuous and lasting voluntary organisation.
2. It has got some aims. Union works for its achievement.
3. It is a union of labour and non-labour employees, who work in various institutes, profession or trade.

4. It tries to improve working conditions of their members. It also tries to maintain their welfare and safeguard their interest.
5. In trade union continuous efforts are being made to regulate relation between workers and owners, owners and owners and workers and workers and make this relation more healthy and meaningful.
6. It represents worker in the discussion regarding working hours, salary, working condition and other matters.
7. It can be a union of workers, owners or independent workers.
8. It works to avail maximum benefits to the workers.
9. Trade unions varies continuously. They vary according to condition, situation and changes of trends.
10. Laski says that problems of trade unions are regarding economic, legal, moral and social factor.
11. Trade unions protects workers and secure them. They improve their wage, working condition and living standard. They give them a special status in industries and society and increased social control in national economic life become partner in it.
12. The trade unions have become an important part of modern industrial society. Previously they were interested only in the benefits of their members only. But nowadays they take interest in social and cultural development of the nation also.
13. They are attached only with financial matters. They protect interest of their members. They constantly try to establish good relation with employer by collective bargaining.

4. TRADE UNIONS AND THEIR FUNCTIONS IN OTHER COUNTRIES

Other Countries

Trade Unionism is an international concept which spread all over the world. Its functions and forms are different nation-wise. The trade unions work according to nation's condition and problems. Function of the trade unions in some nations can be discussed as following :

1. Trade Unions in ex-U.S.S.R. (Russia). The U.S.S.R. which has been divided in various countries now provides some ideals for trade unions. In 1959 trade union act functions of trade unions were narrated as following :

(1) To improve quality of production by increasing productivity of workers.

(2) To revise the wage rates and participate in wage control and planning.

(3) To assist in technical progress.

(4) To make accord by collective bargainings participate in solution of industrial disputes.

(5) To make agreement with owner for due and sufficient use of the fund allotted for industrial and social safety.

(6) Construction of rest houses; to make arrangement for the hygiene of the workers, and give facility of hygiene to women and children.

(7) To raise fund for mutual help.

(8) Scientific and political education should be given to the members to develop social, political and scientific awareness in them; to start activities for production technique.

(9) Development of clubs, libraries and cultural activities and planning of sports and cultural activities for the worker.

(10) To encourage the women to come forward in public life, production line and social life.

(11) To publish labour law circulars, implement and observe them.

(12) To impose discipline in workers.

(13) To provide residential and welfare facilities to the workers.

It is clear from above matters that function of trade unions in Russia is not limited for wages or working condition but it also works for their members overall development. They do many activities to give contribution in national development. Right of going on strike is not raised there and even it is not necessary there.

In Russia, collective bargaining is known as social labour accord, regarding which Alexandar says that...

> The socialistic labour agreement tries to seek participation of workers in friendly collaboration free from exploitation as a worker or an employee, fulfilling a certain labour function in a given socialistic undertaking.

Thus, trade union's activities can be called very good and ideal.

2. Trade Union Activities in China. The Communist China which has a very less effect of global privatisation and market reforms; in this nation there is a special role of trade union with reference to worker and the state. An expert name Wu. Y. narrates function of trade unions as under :

1. To improve physical and cultural standards by starting a campaign for the increase in labour productivity and discipline.
2. To observe the administration for achieving targets of the planning.
3. To conduct political, academic and technical study classes and also to conduct cultural as well as sports activities.

4. To register members, collect funds and report about activities.
5. To make the workers aware about professional skill and current economic and political crises.
6. To provide entertainment to the workers by activities like dance, music, cinema, sports other entertainment instruments and library.
7. To provide same compensation for same work.
8. To guarantee for economic help to the aged, sick and disable workers.
9. To protect women and children from exploitation.
10. To participate in various drive for improving life style of workers.
11. To participate in the activity of collective bargaining for the purpose like wages, working standard, production, labour safety, welfare, social securities etc.

Above matters show that there is a special and important role of trade union activity in China.

3. Trade Union Activities in America. In America trade unions do many work for welfare of their members which can be narrated as following :

1. To protect workers from capitalist exploitation.
2. To improve working condition, to increase wages, and to decrease working hours during lengthy work.
3. To take actions for maintaining enough security during duty hours.
4. To increase share of labourers in national income. For that to implement democratic labour administration and labour laws.
5. To protect labourers from slavery, worst condition and improper behaviour.
6. To provide equal opportunity to all labourers.
7. To support the legal structure, which helps the workers and does not harm them.
8. To preserve democratic institutes and develop them.
9. To boost up global peace and independence.
10. To protect labour activity from corruption and under policies. Similarly, protect it from factors like communism, fascism and dictatorship to encourage opinion of workers.
11. To make efforts so that sale of products manufactured by unions may go high.
12. To develop local institutes and co-operative activities.
13. To participate in administration, discussion and agreement.
14. To participate in welfare and academic activities of society and to join in national activities.

15. To seek protection through social security laws imposed by the state and to provide facilities like housing scheme, radio programme, loan, labour bank, co-operative work, entertainment, pension, medical benefits, insurance etc.

Above matter clearly shows that trade union has special activity in U.S.A. These activities are being performed in such a way that democratic framework develops and independence of the members are preserved.

4. Trade Unions in England. In the British T.U.C. report of post-war reforms, main objects of trade unions have been described as under :

1. To maintain wage, working hours and working condition. Similarly, to increase volume of net national income and to increase contribution of labourers in it.
2. To observe that enough opportunities are given to workers and to make improvement in it so that total employment can be achieved.
3. To make efforts for more labour participation in management, to achieve aims of industries, and contribution of workers may increase.
4. After world war special function of trade unions is represented.

Flanders and Cleg narrates aims of trade unions as under :

1. To preserve and improve wage and working condition.
2. To uplift labourers' status as citizen of society and industry.
3. To expand social control in national fiscal life and to participate in the control.

Prof. Laski says that, nowadays trade unions plays an important role. Their functions are multiple.

In Britain trade union activity is not limited upto wage and working condition, but it also make effort to raise labourer's status in industry and society.

According to *John Price*, "Trade unions of England gives some benefits and they also work for state welfare services. More personal needs are considered. They are accountable to the whole society."

"Trade union improves wage and working conditions at one side on the other side it also make efforts to decrease imbalance between various class of society, improvement in living standard and development of human capacity."

5. FUNCTIONS OF TRADE UNIONS IN INDIA.

Generally, functions of trade unions can be divided into two parts, *viz.* protecting functions and development functions. First type of functions protect labourers against wage, working hours, working condition etc.

And second type of functions include steps for social and cultural development of workers and to take steps for improvement in their status.

Prof. Ghosh says that, "Modern trade unions are interested in problem of productivity, social trends, employment and price expansion." An expert named *Broughton* says that, "In industries the trade unions depend on strikes, discussion or collective bargaining for the labour welfare functions like good working condition, regulation of working hours, sufficient wage, security, education, entertainment, housing facilities, medical facility etc. It also tries for facilities for religious or social functions."

According to *Samual Gomyears* "The trade unions try for safe-guarding interest of workers and their happy life."

According to Trade Union Act, 1926 "The unions must work to protect and promote the interest of the workers and conditions of their employment."

The Indian National Commission for Labour has recommended to give more attention on following trade union functions :

1. The labourer should be given due wages.
2. To improve working condition by maintaining safety.
3. To expand opportunities for promotion and training.
4. Improvement in working condition and living standard.
5. To provide amenities for education, cultural activities and entertainment.
6. To increase various know-hows of labourers and co-operate in technological development.
7. To make efforts for improving labour interest in industry.
8. To provide responsible co-operation for improvement of production, quality of production, discipline and high standard quality.
9. To increase personal and mass welfare.
10. To increase temperament of national unity.
11. To participate in formation and implementation of economic, social polities of society.
12. To create sense of responsibility among workers towards industries and society.

In the documents of First Five Year Plan following matters were suggested :

- to make plans for workers;
- to make wage demands which is appropriate to the social justice and financial need;
- to bear more responsibility for industrial success.

Kennedy has recommended some important standards for Trade Union, which includes:

1. To improve level of labour efforts.
2. Improvement of industrial efficiency for technological improvement by giving liberty to the owners.
3. Absolute reduction in industrial unrest.
4. Demand for wage and relevant benefits.

Thus, trade unions work for industrial peace, maintenance of discipline, support to technological changes and adoption of develop-oriented wage payment.

Thus, it is apparent from above matter that trade unions in India are inclined with important responsible developing activities.

6. INTERNATIONAL OBSERVATION ON THE ROLE OF TRADE UNION

In world's countries trade unions role and contribution are different. In any country contribution of trade unions depend upon that country's economic and social condition, level of industrial development and on the ratio of wage earners.

In capitalist countries trade unions continuously try to protect labourers from capitalist exploitation. In democratic nations trade unions play prime role in implementing government plans, schemes and labour welfare policies. In communist nations their policy depend on state or government.

In France and Netherlands there is a legal provision that discussion should be done with trade unions, while forming financial and social matter laws. In Sweden it participates in planning commission function. They bear responsibility for implementation of social welfare and labour programme. In Germany and Yugoslavia they participate in management. Trade Unions Act has partner of social controls in Britain. There is no well-planned or systematic relation of trade unions with government in America and Australia.

It seems from observation of world trade unions contribution that they do not work only for wage and working conditions but also work for social, political, cultural and all other matters which is concerned with labourers. Thus, today trade unions play an important and decisive role in all over the world.

7. PRINCIPLES REGULATING FUNCTIONS OF TRADE UNION

As contribution of trade unions increase their functions also increase. In this condition it becomes inevitable to regulate their function. Their functions must be regulated so that external elements, politicians, local persons etc. factors may not use them as a tool to fulfil their own narrow and selfish interest. The theories which regulate the functions of trade unions are called theories regulating their function. So many experts and organisations have expressed their views on it.

Sydney Webb says that trade unions should get guidance from the effects caused on national permanent efficiency and not from the result achieved due to improvement of condition in special class of labourers in special condition. Any method of trade unionism due to which less productive tools selected, low level management adopted, less physical utilisation of labourers and such partial benefits achieved are disgusting. On the other side, any trade union can be beneficial to whole nation and society, if they select more productive tools, make more selective use of capital intellect and labour make improvement in ability of intelligent and laborious workers.

From the above viewpoints it is clear what trade unions should do and what they should not. They should not do any such thing which is beneficial to a particular class or community but which is harmful to society or nation. Principles regulating trade unions' function can be narrated as following :

1. The trade unions can achieve their aims through collective bargainings. Collective bargainings depend on demand and supply factor. This principle is very important in context with development of owners unions, development in labour owner relations and changed state's industrial policy.
2. Trade Unions should work so that workers get appropriate wage and right to get wage. Trade Unions should also work so that status of workers is increased in society and life, its efficiency increases and also increase standard of skill which can be useful to industries also.
3. Workers are accepted as partner of industry. So, they should participate in procedure of management. Their participation in management will be more meaningful.
4. Each worker has right for work, to rest, to get compensation at the time of disability, illness and old age and to get same compensation for same work. Workers and owners should try to implement these socialistic principles.
5. *Daker* says that, "Unions aim at securing economic security and betterment, industrial and social status and role as political institution."
6. Trade unions shall be able to safeguard labourers' financial interest only if they are internally strong. They should have full capacity to fight against tremendous power of owners.

7. It should be capable of working as responsible and active unit. It should be aware of opportunity, limitation and alternatives to rectify chance. Its management should be democratic and independent.
8. They should be capable to use best method to achieve their aims. They should try to achieve their aims adopting methods like mutual insurance, collective bargaining, legal provisions, pressures etc.

Above principles clear that how trade unions should work and what they should not do.

REFERENCES

1. Yoder, Dale, *Personnel Management and Industrial Relations*, 1972, pp. 159-160.
2. Punekar, S.D., *Trade Unionism in India*, 1948, p. 1.
3. Webb, Sydney and Beatrice, *History of Trade Unionism*, 1920, p. 1.
4. Cunison, J., *Labour Organisation*, 1930, p. 13.
5. Cole, G.D.H., *An Introduction to Trade Unionism*, p. 13.
6. Barou, N., *British Trade Unions*, pp. 29-30.
7. Richardson, J.H., *An Introduction to the Study of Industrial Relations*, 1961, p. 137.
8. Sloan and Zurcher, *Dictionary of Economics*, 1957, p. 183.
9. Laski, Harold, J., *Trade Unions in the New Society*, 1949, p. 28.
10. Flanders and Clegg, *Systems of Industrial Relations in Great Britain*, p. 192.
11. Mathur, A.S. and J.S. Mathur, *Trade Union Movement in India*, 1957, p. 3.
12. I.L.O., *The Trade Union Situation in U.S.S.R.*, 1960, pp. 96-104.
13. Alexandar, N.G., *Soviet Labour Laws*, p. 168.
14. Wu, Y., *An Economic Survey of Communist China*, 1950.
15. Flanders and Clegg, *System of Industrial Relations in Great Britain*, p. 192.
16. Price, J., *The British Trade Union*, p. 28.
17. I.L.O., *Trade Union Situation in U.K.*, 1961.
18. Ghosh, S., *Trade Unionism in Underdeveloped Countries*, p. 13.
19. Broughton, *Labour in Indian Industries*, 1938, pp. 181-89.
20. Quoted in George Selders, *The Great Quotations*, p. 941.
21. Planning Commission, *The First Five Year Plan*, New Delhi, 1952, pp. 581-82.
22. *Ibid.*
23. Kennedy, Van, D., *Unions, Employers and Government*, Manatatas, Bombay, 1966, pp. 208-13.
24. Webb, Sydney, and Bentrice, *Industrial Democracy*, p. 703.
25. *Ibid.*, p. 574.
26. Daker, C.E., *An Introduction to Labour*.

9

Theoretical and Empirical Analysis on Economic and Social Condition of Female Workers

> "The new industrial organisation made woman an integral part of the new economic order and an important part of its manpower recourse."
>
> —*Klein*

Outline of the Chapter

1. Introduction.
2. Female workers participation.
3. Female workers in unorganised sector.
4. Studies on female workers in unorganised sectors.
5. Division of labour between men and women.
6. Legal protection to female labour.
7. Male-female wage-differentials : Global Scenario.
8. Studies on problems of farm workers.

1. INTRODUCTION

Women play an important role in the development of human society. According to opinion of Swedish Scholar Gustar Geigor, the dignity of women in society provides an exact measure of the development of society. Our late Prime Minister Honurable Jawaharlal Nehru had observed that to awaken the people it is the woman who must be awakened, once she is on the move, the family moves, the village moves, the nation moves.

The father of ethic values, Manu wrote that when women were adored

God's frequented that place. But unfortunately at any time, at any age, women did not enjoy equal and honourable status in her family and society with men. Manu himself wrote that there can be no independence for woman at any stage of her life, that before marriage she must remain under the tutelage of her parents, after marriage under that of her husband and after the death of her husband under that of her children.

The dignity and place of woman deteriorated considerably in "ipic" and "Smriti" periods. Women continued to lose place and dignity at the Rajput and Muslim invaders period. At the time of arriving of Britishers in India, the dignity of women in Indian society had reached its lowest ebb. There are many bad traditions and customs just like child marriage, polygamy, seclusion and purdah brought about a giant degradation and deterioration in the status of women in the society.

But nineteenth century was a century of liberalisation, freedom and equity for women. Many social and economic legislation and reforms enacted by Government. Many philosophers, politicians, reformers, sociologists had tried for social reforms in context of higher dignity, honour and status of women. This movement has further accelerated during the twentieth century. During this century the doors are opened of professions for women due to higher educational facilities for them.

Many factors are responsible for changing the scenario of women's dignity not only in the society but in the economy, politics, professions, etc. Industrialisation, urbanisation, higher female education, evolution and revolutions of new thinking etc., are the major factors for changing the whole scenario.

Kelin[1] said, "The new industrial organisation made women an integral part of the new economic order and an important part of its manpower recourse." Pomilla Kapoor[2] observed, "One of the major consequences of the varied processes of changes operating in the country has been the emancipation of women from the tradition bound ethos."

2. FEMALE WORK PARTICIPATION

During the planning period the numbers of women and participation in work has considerably increased. We can see this phenomenon in the census report of 1991. The provisional number of total workers with rural-urban, male-female break up is given in table No. 1.

TABLE 1

Total Number of Workers in India*

Population/ Workers (1)	Persons (2)	Males (3)	Females (4)
Population	836,605,522	433,791,705	402,813,817
Workers**	314,903,642	223,506,153	91,397,489
Population/ Workers (1)	Persons (2)	Males (3)	Females (4)
Percentage of Workers	37.64	51.52	22.69
Rural			
Population	621,267,297	320,066,940	301,204,357
Workers**	249,33,072	167;822,985	81,507,087
Percentage of Workers	40.13	52.43	27.06
Urban			
Population	215,338,225	113,728,765	101,609,460
Workers**	65,573,570	55,683,768	9,890,402
Percentage of Workers	30.45	48.96	9.73

* Excludes Jammu and Kashmir

**Workers include both main workers and marginal workers.

Source : Census of India, 1991, Paper 3 of 1991.

Here we can see that the numbers of female workers are less than male workers. It is more lower in urban as compared to rural area. Table No. 2 shows the work participation rate in India.

TABLE 2

Work Participation Rate : 1981-1991

Year	Workers	Per cent	Males	Females
1981	Total	36.70	52.62	19.67
	Rural	38.79	53.77	23.06
	Urban	29.99	49.06	8.31
1991	Total	37.68	51.56	22.73
	Rural	40.24	52.50	27.20
	Urban	30.44	48.95	9.74

Note : Excludes Assam and J & K.

Source : Census of India, 1991, Paper 3 of 1991.

It can be seen from this table that the rate of work participation of male has been slightly declined in 1991 compared to 1981, whereas it has been increased for females.

Most of the female workers are engaged in unorganized sector, women engaged in different sectors. Table No. 3 shows women labour in primary, secondary and tertiary sectors.

TABLE 3

Women Labour in Different Sectors

Industrial Categories	Percentage distribution of female main workers	
(A) Primary Sector	1971	1981
1. Cultivators	29.84	33.20
2. Agricultural Labourers	50.86	45.18
3. Livestock, Forestry, Fishing etc.	1.76	1.06
4. Mining & Quarrying	0.40	0.36
Total	82.86	79.80
(B) Secondary Sector		
5. Manufacturing, Processing, Servicing and repairs		
(i) Household Industry	4.24	4.59
(ii) Other than Household Industry	2.77	3.55
6. Construction	0.65	0.80
Total	7.66	8.94
(C) Tertiary Sector		
7. Trade and Commerce	1.78	2.04
8. Transport, Storage and Communication	0.47	0.38
9. Other Services	7.08	7.05
Total	9.33	9.74

Here in this table we can observe the shift of women labourers from the Primary Sector to Secondary and Tertiary Sectors.

3. FEMALE WORKERS IN UNORGANISED SECTOR

We have come to know from census statistical profile that most of the female workers are unorganised. In nowadays, it is an academic fashion to use this term unorganised. Everyday using this term in general, therefore, there is wide confusion about its interpretation. Let we first clarify this term.

Deepak Mazumdar[3] explained that entry into the information sector labour market is unrestricted while that in the formal sector labour markets restricted by artificially raised hiring standards, norms and procedures.

According to the interpretation of Central Statistical Organisation, the organised sector comprises units registered under the Factory Acts of 1948 and covers those using power and employing 10 or more workers, moreover, those units not using power but employing 20 or more workers. The organised sector managed by specific certain laws such as minimum wages acts, labour welfare legislation, The Contract Labour (Regulation and Abolition) Act, etc.

On the other front the unorganised sector includes agriculture cottage and tiny industry, the service sector of domestic work, unregistered factories etc. These sectors are not found to implement laws and legislation.

The National Commission on Labour narrated the following characteristics to unorganised sector :

(a) Small size of establishments with low investment per employed person.
(b) Casual nature of employment.
(c) Ignorance and illiteracy.
(d) Scattered nature of establishments.
(e) Superior strength of employers operating singly and in combination.

The ILO-UNDP mission to Kenya (1972) mentioned the following characteristics of the informal sectors :

1. Case of entry of new enterprise.
2. Family ownership.
3. Small size of operation.
4. Unregulated and competitive market.
5. Labour intensive technology.
6. Informally acquired skills of workers through the job training.
7. No state support.
8. Deplorable working conditions and low wages.

From above description we can clearly define and interpret the term "Unorganised Sector". As we know, most of the female workers in unorganised sectors, just like farm sector, construction, cottage industry, domestic home-based services etc.

Most of female workers are either illiterate or lower education.

Therefore, they have to work in low paid and low skilled jobs. According to 1981 census, 80 per cent of the women workers are in agriculture, constituting 87 per cent rural areas and 17.5 per cent in urban areas.

Ambannavar[4] wrote that the failure of structural change in employment to accompany urbanisation can be traced to the fact that the growth of modern industry in towns and cities dealt a death blow to rural household industry.

Laurdes[5] observed that during initial stages of development, the type of industries that are established, mainly textile and leather are labour intensive and provide employment to male bias. Ester Boserup[6] also opined that the female displacement through mechanisation and industrialisation means not only a less of income but loss of social status.

Harish[7] pointed out that there are certain factors which have affected adversely the role of women in our economy are the gradually declined in handicrafts. Another factors are increasing pressure on agriculture increasing rural poverty resulting in migration, development of modem industry with modernisation and mechanisation, the growth of education and the increasing cost of living particularly in urban centres.

Mourya[8] explained the process and problems of urbanisation that urban points have always been treated the nucleus of human civilisation. Yet, they have their own existence, nature, origin and growth for the functions they observed themselves as well as for the areas surrounding them. It is native type and variety of occupations make them distinct from the rural areas.

4. STUDIES ON FEMALE WORKERS IN UNORGANISED SECTORS

Many scholars, researchers, Research/Academic/ Labour institutions and experts have made studies on female workers engaged in unorganised sectors. Few of them can be narrated very briefly as under :

1. Lakdawala and others[9] concluded that in Bombay, employment opportunity were limited for women. These occupations did not require much education, skill and training. Professional occupations were second in importance for women. Although, in these professional occupations women are concentrated in lower grade.
2. According to Sharma[10] out of total urban working women, 75 per cent were concentrated in only 19 occupations. Apart from clerks, teachers and nurses whose percentage was only 20 per cent of total urban female workers the remaining were in occupations which required little or no education. 25 per cent female urban workers were unskilled labourers or domestic servants.

3. Singh and De'Souza[11] concluded that women workers were invariably domestic servants, hawkers, construction workers and petty traders.
4. National Institute of Urban Affairs[12] concluded that in urban areas nearly 40 per cent of the women employed are in services, followed by 30 per cent in trade, 15 per cent in manufacturing, 8 per cent in construction and 5 per cent in primary activities.
5. Thippiah[13] had studied the informal sector units of Bangalore Metropolitan area and concluded that women labourers are suffering from poverty, unemployment in secure employment, exploitation, harassment etc.
6. Ministry of Labour, Government of India[14] holds study on socio-economic conditions of female labourers of building and construction industry. According to this study female labourers of unorganised sector suffer from disabilities and exploitation of higher magnitude than those employed in the organised sector.
7. Mathur[15] concluded that there were constant problems of instability and insecurity for the women workers engaged in construction industry.
8. Lal Das[16] studied the female workers in unorganised construction sector of Andhra Pradesh. He concluded that development has improved the standard of living but increased economic and social disparities.
9. Kaptan[17] holds a case study of Amravati City regarding the income, wages and working conditions of female labourers in unorganised sector and concluded that the social conditions in which they live continue to be traditional exploitative and anti-women in nature.

5. DIVISION OF LABOUR BETWEEN MEN AND WOMEN

We can see the division of labour between men and women in our labour market. Henry Phels[18] observed that "Workers who are distinguished by some characteristics (such as sex, caste, status etc.) that does not affect their present capacity but are treated less favourably in given employment than others who are of no greater capability but are not marked off by the characteristics."

Ester Boserup[19] explain the division of labour between male and female very deeply and widely. He wore, "the division of labour according to sex is often explained as a natural result of physiological and psychological differences between men and women. But apart from the obvious case of child bearing there are extremely few convincing examples of sex division of labour being truly explicable in term of natural differences between men and women. This is apparent when the sex-pattern of work in different parts of the world are compared. In different human communities, quite different tasks are labelled as male and female tasks.

To be an independent farmer is a male task in India and in Europe, but in many other regions it is normal occupation for a woman to farm on her own account and perform all the manual labour needed on a plot of land without any male assistance."

He further pointed out that "... The idea that the specialisation of the labour market in male and female tasks is related to natural difference between the sexes is proved wrong when we make a comparison between labour markets in different parts of the world... Clearly the key to understanding these patterns is in the field of culture rather than in human physiology or anatomy."

He further observed that, "Both in primitive and in more developed communities the traditional division of labour within the farm family is usually considered 'natural' in the sense of being obviously and originally imposed by the sex difference itself. But while the members of any given community may think that their particular division of labour between sexes is the 'natural' one because it has undergone little completely different ways of dividing the burden of work among the sexes and they may find their ways just as 'natural'. Africa is the region of female farming *par excellence*... in India too many examples of female farming system are known. They are found with women working more hours in farming than men."

Bipal Dasgupta[20] observed that there are villages just like in Muzinga and Tanzania, where sex specification of jobs are nearly complete, on the other had there are other types of villages just like in Nepal and Mexico where jobs are interchangeable. Joyce Labraet[21] explained this approach in the context of Japan, "The unprecedented changes in the Japanese countryside over the past two decades have dramatically transformed the lives of rural women... one of the most important changes affecting in the lives of the farm women lies in the nature of their work. In the space of ten of fifteen years, women labourers have replaced their husbands and sons as major workers and even managers for their families farms. With an ever increasing number of rural men engaged in non-farm work, Japanese farming, long characterised as 'family-farming' has become 'female-farming' and women who comprise over fifty per cent of agriculture and work force have emerged as the mainstay, of Japanese agriculture."

Alva Myrdol and Viola Klein[22] concluded in their study that, transplantation of seedlings usually performed by women is a tough job. The women frequently having to stand in water, six inches deep, moving backwards in the bending posture as they transplant the seedlings for eight hours a day is no doubt a tough job. The bundles of seedlings pulled out from the nurseries need to be transplanted with minimum delay.

Joyce Lebra *et al.*[23] explained the same from their study that transplanting is a very messy and back breaking job and as one has to stand in mud and slough for hours together in rain and sun. It is particularly hurting to move backwards whole transplanting and one can easily catch cold, being exposed for long hours in such surroundings and the higher caste women do not possess skill to transplants. Main job of scheduled caste women is transplanting. The success of a Paddy crop depends on how well it is transplanted.

Donald R. Michelwail *et al.*[24] studied the role of women in rural development in seven countries of Latin America. This study concluded that, "Division of labour in the fields has begun to break down in Kenya, thanks to the introduction of cash crops and the demands for male labourer in heavily settled areas of the country. Kikiya women have increasingly taken on farming responsibilities formerly held by their husbands, including hoeing, sowing, weeding and harvesting or cash crops. A breakdown in division of labour similar to that in Kenya is occurring in lesotho, where male migration to South Africa is so heavy that women perform traditionally male tasks out of economic necessity... In Peru a rural woman may assume all agricultural chores during the early years of marriage when her husband may migrate to the coast in search of greater economic opportunity."

Sarathi Achharya[25] stated that in South Asian sub-continent more women are employed in rice growing farms. The landless poor females performed all farm works including ploughing but female workers getting a quarter to a third less than men wages. In Phillipine, subsitence-based modern typical faming, skilled jobs reserved for men and intensive farm works for women. In Central Luzon, in transplanting, 99 per cent of the female labour is hired and for harvesting 91 per cent is hired.

Balaraman, S.N.[26] opined that sex discrimination in farm wages is a fact of life in the world's countries. It has existed in two forms, the first one is paying less to women for the same type of work which he calls open discrimination and second is restricting women to low paid unskilled jobs denying them access to better paid jobs.

K. Sardamani[27] concluded in her study on women's involvement in rice production that, women are engaged in production and processing of rice and it is quite difficult to find a rigid sexual division in the tasks performance.

6. LEGAL PROTECTION TO FEMALE LABOUR

According to article 14 of our constitution right to equality has been recognised. This means, state shall not deny to any person equality before the law. According to article 15 the state shall not discriminate against any person on the grounds of race, religion, caste, sex, place of birth etc. But particularly unorganised female labourers engaged in construction, cottage industry, beedi making, basket making, handicraft and handlooms sector, agriculture, dairying, small animal, husbandry, fisheries, social and agro forestry etc. becomes a victim of over-exploitation.

The report of the core group[28] observed that female are discriminated in comparison to males in context of wages, working conditions. Females obtained only half of the wages of males for full day work. Their productivity is same as male workers. This is because wages payable to the women workers are not determined by economic criteria rather it is based on certain other factors *viz.*, cultural attitudes, social practice and power structure in society.

According to the report of the National Commission on employed women that the 94 per cent of the total female work force has been employed in the unorganised sector where their exploitation is maximum in terms of long hours of work, skills, low productivity and lack of job security.

National Commission on Labour[29] stated that women constituted 59.4 millions which constituted approximately 33.10 per cent of the total labour force as per census data of 1961 and during a span of 60 years since the beginning of 20th century their strength in proportion to total labour force had varied between 23.30 per cent to 33.70 per cent and most of females engaged in unorganised sector.

It was observed by the committee on the status of women in India[30] that more than 75 per cent of people live in rural areas and they are mainly engaged in the profession of agriculture and out of total female working force at least 81 per cent of them are engaged in agriculture and otherwise 94 per cent of the women being engaged in the unorganised sector of economy.

Ramesh Chand *et al.*[31] concluded that employment of female labourers depends upon pattern and intensity of crops, nature and level of mechanisation involved quantum of yield of each crop etc. Due to highly mechanisation there is less employment of female workers. This study observed that in Punjab, the pattern of employment of male and female workers has changed significantly due to cumulative effect of certain factors such as modernisation, increase in irrigation facilities, cropping factor and intensity.

Arputhamurth Savitri[32] pointed out that the high yielding variety of crop technology in isolation increase the demand for female labour particularly in paddy crop as compared to wheat crop due to the fact that it needs a new package of practising requiring much cure of labour consequently there accrues an urgent need of casually hired labour due to certain time bound activities such as fertilisers application, weeding and harvesting.

Let us examine the Government's efforts towards female labour. The Seventh Five Year Plan was emphasised for equity and empowerment for the female workers. Government of India have introduced more than 27 schemes for women's certain specific programmes to be implemented by the department of women and child development for betterment of female workers.

The Supreme Court of India in case of state of Madhya Pradesh *Vs.* Promod Bhartiya and others observed that constitutional approach of equal pay of equal work would not come within the Article 14 of Constitution as an abstract doctrine but this rule was nothing but an facet of article 14.

The Supreme Court in another case titled, Surendra Singh *Vs.* Engineer-in-Chief has again emphasised the rule of equal pay for equal work and has disapproved the action of the State Government in disturbing parity.

The President of India promulgated an ordinance called the Equal Remuneration Ordianance, 1975 on 26th Sept. 1975 aiming to implement the spirit of the narration in article 39. Subsequently the equal Remuneration Act, 1976 replaced the above ordinance and implemented in the year 1976. This Act includes : (1) objects and reasons, (2) scope of the Act, (3) definition of important terms, (4) overriding effect of the Act, (5) payment of equal remuneration to men and women workers, (6) no discrimination between men and women workers while recruiting them, (7) role of the Advisory Committee, etc.

According to Fair Wages Committee when "male work" and "female work" classified, there is justification for paying different wages to males and females. It suggested that the wages of female workers should be calculated on the basis of smaller family than that of male workers.

7. MALE-FEMALE WAGE DIFFERENTIALS : GLOBAL SCENARIO

(1) Male-female wage differentials is a world-wide phenomenon. American woman face discrimination of the job. According to U.S. Bureau of Census in 1980, median income of white males was of 13,328 $ and of white females of 4947 dollars. This

was of 8009 dollars of black males and of 4580 dollars of black females. This suggested deeper wage differentials in America. The female labour force participation has considerably increased to 51.6 per cent in 1981 from 37.7 per cent in 1966[33] but females earning remained far behind than males. From 1955 to 1985, women who worked full time the year round earned about 60 per cents to every dollar men working year round, full time earned.[34]

(2) The Soviet Labour Code of 1922 and the constitutions of 1935 and 1978 firmly guaranteed to women for equal pay for equal work. ... labour force participation of women of prime working age, between 20 and 40, has sometime been close to 90 per cent... The proportion of women in transportation in construction and in socialist agriculture are 24, 29 and 44 per cent respectively. Moreover, 7 out of 10 physicians are women. 4 out of 10 engineers are again women.[35] But females earnings is relatively less that of males. Most of the women are engaged low paid occupations. According to estimate, earning ratio of the USSR was 70.0 between 1960 and 1980.[36] In the mid 1960s the gross earnings of women in Soviet Agriculture were between 55 per cent and 70 per cent those of men.[37]

(3) In Sweden antidiscrimination legislation and the Act of equality between men and women was passed in 1980. Sweden is the first country of the world which succeeded in rapidly reducing the earning gap between male and female. The hourly wages of women in industry has risen to 90 per cent of those of men. The ratio of the annual earnings of all full time year round female to male workers was only 81.2 per cent of men in 1980.

(4) In Belgium, anti-discriminatory laws (1978) relating to employed women has been promoted equality in working conditions, wages, employment, promotion, self-employment, vocational guidance, training etc. According to this law, "equality of treatment as between men and women should ensure the absence of any discrimination based on sex either directly or indirectly by reference, *inter-alia*, to marital or family status.

(5) Above type of law enforced in Denmark on 12 April, 1978. According to this Act, every employer to treat men and women alike for the purpose of employment.

(6) Same type of laws were enforced in Germany, Greece, Netherlands, United Britain, Australia, New Zealand, Malaysia, Sri Lanka and many other countries.

8. STUDIES ON PROBLEMS OF FARM WORKERS

There are various studies based on problems of farm workers. It has been broadly classified into three sub-parts. (A) Employment, Problems, (B) Earning Problems, (C) Problems of Lower Standard of living.

Female labourers are an integral and important segment of total farm labour force, these problems are more serious for them. They have to face more serious problems of wages, employment and standard of living. Let us briefly examine the studies on problems of farm workers.

(A) Employment Problems

1. Agrawal C.D.[38] observed that the pattern of farm employment is decided according to (a) Size of farms, (b) Nature of crops grown, (c) Conditions of family and (d) Social attitudes to farm jobs in the farming community.
2. Rajni V. Sundra[39] concluded that the agricultural labourers without land could not obtain regular employment all the year round, due to lack of adequate opportunities of gainful employment, on an average male agricultural labourer was employed for 141.20 days during the year. In case of female, she got employment for 73.20 days in a year of which agricultural work accounted for 68 days.
3. Goswamin, P.C and C.K. Bara[40] concluded that in the case of landless and non-farming families, the problem of surplus labour was more acute.
4. Shah and Singh[41] concluded that in North-West U.P. the employment of both casual and permanent labour was about fifty per cent higher on progressive medium (10 to 30 hectare) and progressive large farms (about 30 hectare) as compared to less progressive farms. Similarly tractor operated progressive farms employed more labour as compared to non-progressive farms.
5. Memoria, C.B.[42] reported that the seasonal character of agricultural operations has resulted in an uneven distribution of labour power. There are particularly two periods when agricultural labour is completely out of work, *i.e.*, from middle of April to the middle of July.
6. Sharma, Singh and Gangwar[43] stated that the majority of labour force was employed for less than 120 days during the six months under reference. About 35 per cent and 60 per cent of agricultural workers were underemployed in Kernal and Mahaindergarh districts respectively.
7. Grewal, R.S. and Singh, Parmatma[44] observed that on an average, a farm worker got work hardly for 65 days on the marginal farms and 126 days on the small farms in a year. It was also revealed that the majority of the farmers faced problems of

adequate employment, non-availability of better breeds of mulch cattle and marketing problems.

(B) Earnings Problems

1. Shah, S.L. and Singh[45] reported that the high yielding varieties programme, has increased the demand for labour but the wage rate has not risen as the supply of labour is quite elastic. It is also expressed that technology and farm income have significant impact on the demand for labour.
2. Ram, G.S. and Singh, C.B.[46] concluded that the annual earnings of an agricultural labour in Uttar Pradesh amounted to Rs. 250 in comparison to Rs. 2200 in Ferojpur. The analysis suggested that the statutory safeguard in terms of minimum wage is not effective proposition for the fate of farm workers.
3. Kawadia Ganesh[47] concluded that the higher rate of increase in high money wage crops zones and lower rate of increase in low wage crop zone have resulted in greater disparity in the wage rates in different crop zones. Normally wheat producing area have higher growth in money wages than the rice producing areas. Thus, the green revolution has increased reasonal disparity in wages for the weaker section in the state.
4. Reddy, Y.V.R., and Rastogi, B.K.[48] observed that the payments are higher for male workers as they attended to semi-skilled works. The wages were higher for male workers as compared to female workers for harvesting of crops which indicates the discrimination in wage payments. It was also observed that the wages for some of the non-agricultural works were relatively higher than the agricultural works. The problems of unemployment and low wages affect the economic condition and standard of living of agricultural labourers.

(C) Problems of Lower Standard of Living

1. Iyanger[49] concluded that the proportion of annual consumption was found low in families with a higher annual income. The marginal propensity to consume and income elasticity of consumption was worked out of 6.52 and 0.51 respectively.
2. Singh, R.D. and others[50] found in their study that over 46 per cent households were below the poverty line. In the case of the landless agricultural labourers and the marginal farmers, these figures came to 58.6 per cent and 63.3 per cent respectively of their respective households.
3. Sharma, Nandlal and Bhan Chandra[51] stated that all the 50 (fifty) sample households were observed under debt. If per capita monthly income of Rs. 40, at current prices, is taken as the

base for minimum standard of living, all the 50 landless labourer families were found below poverty line.

4. Singh, R.D. and others[52] observed that 60 per cent of the landless labourers and 58 per cent of marginal farmers were in debt as compared to 57 per cent of small, 42 per cent of medium and 33 per cent of large farmers.
5. Ghose, M.G.[53] concluded that the conditions of the agricultural labourers were worse off than that of marginal farmers. They were not only poor, but their conditions had deteriorated during the past decade.

Above all description throws the light on problem of agricultural labourers. These problems are more serious for female labourers. Here, we can conclude that economic and social condition of female workers is pitiable and more serious. They have a problems of lower employment, wages, earnings, lower standard of living, hard work, fatigue, poor working conditions, lower social status etc.

REFERENCES

1. Klein quoted in Lalitha Devi, *Status and Employment of Women in India*, B.R. Publishing Corporation, Delhi, 1982, p. 16.
2. Kapoor, Promilla, *Marriage and the Working Women*, p. 3.
3. Mazumdar, D., quoted in Tripathy, S.N. and Saudaminidas, *Informal Labour Women in India*, Discovery Publishing House, New Delhi, 1991.
4. Ambannavar, J.P., *Demography India*, Vol. 4, December 1975, pp. 344-346.
5. Laurdes, A., *Women in the Informal Sector and National Development : The Complexities of Change* (ed.), Wellesly Editorial Committee, University of Chicago Press, 1977, pp. 28-9.
6. Ester Bosrup, *Women's Role in Economic Development*, 1970, pp. 139-46.
7. Harish, *Economic Development and Role of Indian Woman*, Commonwealth Publishers, New Delhi, p. 92.
8. Mourya, S.D., *Urban Environment Management : A Functional Study*, Chugh Publications, Allahabad, 1988.
9. Lakdawala, D.T. and others, *Work, Wages and Well-being in an Indian Metropolis*, Bombay, 1963, p. 376.
10. Sharma, O.P., "Occupational Structure of Urban Working Woman", *The Economic Times*, 1975.
11. Singh, A.M., and De'Souza, A., *Slum and Pavement Dwellers in the Major Cities of India*, Indian Social Institute, NIMCO, 1977, p. 91.
12. (Quoted by) Tripathi, S.N. and Saudamini Das, *Informal Women Labour in India*, New Delhi, 1991, p. 23.
13. Thippiah, P., "Women Workers in Unorganised Sector", *Social Welfare*, Vol. XXXVI, No. 2, May 1989, pp. 21-22.
14. Ministry of Labour, Government of India, New Delhi.
15. Mathur, R.N., *Quality of Working Life of Women Construction Workers*, Commonwealth Publishers, New Delhi, p. 45.

16. Das Lal, D.K., *Sex Discrimination against Female Workers in Unorganised Sector*, Commonwealth Publishers, New Delhi.
17. Kaptan, S.S., "The Income, Wages and Working Condition of Women Workers in Urban Unorganised Sector, A Case Study of Amravati City", *Social Welfare*, Vol. XXXVI, No. 2, 1979.
18. Henry, Phels Brown, *The Pay Inequality*, Oxford University Press, Walton Street, Oxford, 1977, p. 145.
19. Ester, Boserup, "The Traditional division of Work between Sexes" a source of unequality-women in the labour market, Research Series No. 21, July to August, 1984, p. 1.
20. Bipal, Dasgupta, *et al.*, *Village Society and Labour Use*, Oxford University Press, New Delhi, 1978, p. 43.
21. Joyce, Lebra, *et al.*, (editors), *Women in Changing Japan*, Standard University Press, California, 1978, p. 40.
22. Alva, Myrdol and Viola Klein, *Women's Two Roles*, Routledge Keganpaul Limited, 1970, p. 5.
23. Joyce, Lebra, *et al.*, *Women and Work in India*, Okhla Industrial Area, New Delhi, 1984, pp. 69-72.
24. Donald. R. Michelwail, *et al.*, *Women and Rural Development*, West View Press, Boulder, Colorada, p. 34.
25. Sarthi, Achharya, Women and Rural Development in the Third World, Paper presented in the workshop on, "Women, Technology and Forms of Production", on 30th and 31st October, 1984, p. 45 conducted by Madras Institute of Development Studies, Madras.
26. Balaram, S.N., "Sex Discrimination in Farm Wages in Tamilnadu", *Indian Journal of Agricultural Economics*, Vol. XL, No. 3, Conference Number, July-September 1985.
27. K. Sardamani, "Labour, Land and Rice-Production (Women's Involvement in Three States)", *Economic and Political Weekly*, Vol. XXII, No. 17, April 25, 1987, pp. 252-56.
28. Report of the Core Group on "National Perspective Plan for Women, 1988-2000" Set up by the Department of Women and Child Development, Ministry of Human Resource Development, Govt. of India, 1988.
29. Report of the National Commission on Labour, Para. 27.4, at 380, 1968.
30. Towards Equality : Report of the Committee on the Status of Women in India, 1974, p. 157.
31. Ramesh Chand, D.S. Sindhu and J.L. Kaul, "Impact of Agricultural Modernisation on Labour-use pattern in Punjab with special reference to women labour", *Indian Journal of Agriculture Economics*, Vol. XI, No. 3, Conference No. 1985.
32. Arputhamurthy, Savitri, *Women, Work and Discrimination*, Ashish Publication, 1990.
33. Nancy, S. Burrett, "Obstacles to Economic Parity of Women", *The American Economic Review*, Vol. 72, No. 2, May, 1982, pp. 160-165.
34. Francine, D. Balu, and Marianne, A. Ferber, *The Economics of Women, Men and Work*, Prentice Hall, Englewood Cliffs, New Jersey, 1986, p. 170.
35. Francine, D. Balu, and Marianne A. Ferber, *op. cit.*, p. 335.
36. *Ibid.*, p. 336.
37. Alaistair, Mcayley, *Women's Work and Wages in the Soviet Union*, George Allen and Unwin, London, 1981, p. 102.

38. Agrawal, C.D., "Pattern of Employment of Hired Labour in Agriculture", *Indian Journal of Agricultural Economics*, Vol. XII, April to June, 1957, p. 34.
39. Rajan, V. Sundra, "Employment and Earnings of Hired Labour in Agriculture", *Indian Journal of Agriculture Economics*, Vol. XII, April to June, 1957, p. 43.
40. Goswami, P.C., and Bara, C.K., "Demand for Labour in Rural Areas", *Indian Journal of Agriculture Economics*, Vol. XXV, No. 3, 1970, p. 22.
41. Shah and Singh, "The Impact of New Agricultural Technology on Rural/Employment in North-West U.P." *Indian Journal of Agriculture Economics*, 25(3), 1970, pp. 29-33.
42. Mamoria, C.B., "Rural Unemployment", *Agriculture Problems in India*, Chapter 17, 1973, p. 385.
43. Sharma, Raj, K.P. Singh and A.C. Gangwar, "Employment. Wages and Mobility of Rural Labour in Haryana", *Indian Journal of Agriculture Economics*, 29(3), 1974, pp. 68-69.
44. Grewal, R.S. and Singh Parmatma, "Prospects and Problems of Marginal and Small Farmers in Haryana", *Indian Journal of Agriculture Economics*, Vol. XXX (3), 1975, p. 257.
45. Shah S.L. and Singh, "Impact of New Technology on Rural Employment", *Indian Journal of Agriculture Economics*, Vol. XXV, July to September 1970, p. 29.
46. Ram, G.S. and Singh, C.B., "Wages and Employment of Agricultural Labourers in U.P. and Punjab", *Indian Journal of Agriculture Economics*, Vol. XXIX (3), 1974, July to Sept. p. 67.
47. Kawadia, Ganesh. "Wages of Weaker Section in M.P.", *Indian Journal of Agriculture Economics*, Vol. XXXV(4), 1980, p. 95.
48. Reddy, Y.V.R. and Rastogi, B.K. "A Study on Employment, Earnings and Standard of Living of Agricultural Labourer in Dryland Areas in Hyderabad Region", *Agro-Economic Research in Drought-Prone Areas, Co-ordination Cell, Dryland Agriculture*, (ICAR), Hyderabad, p. 19.
49. Iyanger, S. Kesva, *Rural Economic Survey*, Hyderabad State, Government Press, 1951, Hyderabad.
50. Singh, R.D. and Others, *Comparative Economic Study on Marginal Farmers and Landless Agricultural Labourers in Ballia District of U.P.*, Division of Agriculture Economics, U.P. Agriculture University, Pantnagar, 1972, p. 32.
51. Sharma, M.L., Nandal and Bhan Chandra, "Green Revolution and Changing Trends in Wage Structure of Landless Labourers in Rural Hissar (Haryana)", *Indian Journal of Agriculture Economics*, Vol. XXIX(3), 1974, p. 69.
52. Singh, R.D. and others, *Comparative Economic Study on Marginal Farmers and Agricultural Labourers* in Ballia District of U.P. Agriculture University, Pantnagar, 1972, p. 103.
53. Ghose, M.G., "The Problems and Prospects of Marginal Farmers and Agricultural Labourers in West Bengal", *Indian Journal of Agriculture Economics*, Vol. XXIX (3), 1974, p. 77.

10

Problems of Female Workers

"The dignity of women in society provides an exact measure of the development of society."

—*Gustar Geigor*

Outline of the Chapter

1. Analysis of Research on Problems of Female Labourers.
2. Characteristics of Female Agricultural Labourers.
3. Problems of Female Agricultural Labourers.

In these days responsibility of women is not limited. Not only she contributes to household activities, not she also contributes to economic activity *e.g.* agriculture sector and animal husbandry at the same time contribution of women is important in fisheries. It is desired that this contribution from women in the economic activities increases. For this there are three reasons, First, Status of a working women is better, Two, this increases the income of household and three, female labour is an important part of total human workforce.[1] They work in all kinds of economic activity. As the number of women workforce increases, national and international level organisations make force to develop an ideology, planning, etc. specified for women. They change the conditions of employment, working conditions, working hours, etc. International Labour Organisation suggests and recommends its member-nations to implement the changes morally for women workers. International Labour Organisation has suggested several important resolutions like maternity, security, women working during the night and underground or in mining,[2] working conditions, hours of work and wage related things. India has adopted almost all the resolutions given by the International Labour Organisation. But still female workers are suffering from several problems despite the efforts of ILO and its implementation by government of India. Working hours, conditions of work, terms, types of job and other situation is still not favourable to women workers. Unorganised labour has still many problems and the problems of unorganised women labour are more serious and severe.

1. ANALYSIS OF RESEARCH ON PROBLEMS OF FEMALE LABOURERS

Analysis of researches on problems of female labourers will be helpful to understand the problems faced by women workers.

Inclusion of women in employment is increasing. The inclusion is more in rural areas than the urban areas but still the level is negligible compared to the involvement of male in the employment. According to 1961 census, 34 women per 100 were working and there were 55 working males per 100. In 1971 census 12 women and 53 males were working per 100 women and males respectively. According to 27th round of NSS in Gujarat, employment inclusion rate for male and female is 53.1 and 36.1 respectively.[3] Most of the females work in the primary sector. According to 1961 and 1971 census, 90 and 94 per cent of working females were engaged in primary sector respectively.[4] Ninety per cent of female labour works on daily wages basis which is irregular and not safe. Some of the problems of female labour is concerned with this factor.

A. Imbalance in the supply of female labours

Female labour is not a main person in her household who goes for work. They work as an additional income earner for the family. Thus, their supply is not continuous and balanced. Most of the times when income of a family is not sufficient, women is allowed to work. When the income increases women is asked to stop the work. Thus, resulting in imbalanced supply of female labourers. Sometimes supply line of female labour bands backward or turns in that direction, it has been observed. This signifies that when the average wage rate decreases, supply of female labour increases (because income of family decreased) and when the average wage rate increases supply of female labour decreases.

In season, supply of female labour is more and when there is off-season, supply of women workers is very less. Thus, supply of female labourers is imbalanced, at the same time most of the female labour do not prefer to work outstation.[5]

B. Female Employment and its Effect on Family Activities

If a female gets an employment she still has to manage the daily family affairs. She has to look after children and older members of the family. She has to go in market for shopping and be present in all the social gatherings. If a female gets an employment, there can be effect on daily family life. Thus, she has to devote time from leisure or family life to its working.

There is adverse effect of female work on its family life. Household work has to be done though a male. Where women goes for work male has to participate in the family activities.

Husband helps wife in family activity and has to clean dishes.[6] Thus, there is a direct effect of women's work to her daily family activity Scenes of husband's helping wife is more often in Western countries. But in India women has to do the family activities. Only due to poor family background or in case of inadequate family income women is allowed to work.

C. Wage Related Problems

Women works to increase the income of the family or widow works for self-dependence. Number of women working only for hobby or to get an employment is very less in India.[7] Thus, wage rates they are getting is an important factor to be considered. Most significant problems of female labourers are problems related to wages. Females get less as compared to males. There is difference between wages of male and female working in same kind of environment and doing the same kind of work. Females do get less in wages, as their kind of job is different. They work in less important or primary sectors, where the possibility of getting good wages is less. For less wages given to female labour social and traditional system is responsible. International Labour Organisation in its special report on why women gets less wages quotes that only constant factor affects the female labour wage rate. That factor in male is reference to women in training. For this there are two reasons : There are inadequate facility for training of women and women is less interested in increasing its skills. Traditional sectors in which women works is below standars.[8] It is understandable that women gets low wages in traditional sectors. In the countries where there is no specific standard of wage range, there is the same situation prevailing. Committee on Textile Industry of Bombay Government[9] has reported this in its report, "Problems of women labour should be examined differently. Australia, Canada and America has decided on minimum or basic wage rate for women. Their evaluation standards are different from male labourers." But, a committee favoured the low wage rate for women workers engaged in road construction and building construction, 1948. Women are being paid less compared to male labour is beneficial to female labourers otherwise they would be out of job."[10] It means, if women and men are being paid same for the same kind of job then the productivity of female labourers is less, owners believe, compared to that of male labourer. This belief is logical but not desired. In a judgement to Madras Cotton Textile Mill, Judge observed that, "Female is being paid less in wages compared to male. This difference is not desired. There is no reason to pay less to women. There should be equal wage rate for men and women."[11] But still, actually women are being paid less than men. Principle of same wage rate for same job is not implemented practically.

2. CHARACTERISTICS OF FEMALE AGRICULTURAL LABOURERS

There are different types of labourers who earn and fulfil the basis requirements of family by doing different type of work or job. They possess different types of characteristics. All the workers have different types of problems, work type and specific working style. Most of the workers earn through physical activity. On the basis of sex labourers can be divided in two groups, male labourers and female labourers. Female labourers work in all sectors, at the same time female also work in agricultural sector. Characteristics of female agricultural workers can be listed as below :

1. Female agricultural labourers are semi-skilled. The work they do in the field do not require specific skills. Here they require only physical work ability. In other fields also female labourers are unskilled or semi-skilled such as construction where female labourers are unskilled. Some sectors do require skills. Female labourers in agricultural sector are semi-skilled because they do not perform duties involving skill like, handling of machinery, etc.
2. They have to work in open, thus seasonal changes do affect their work. They do perform works involving hard physical work. Female agricultural labourers are found to be illiterate. There is a danger of accident in the work they perform. They do not prefer to move out to urban areas if they get opportunity to work in rural areas.
3. Female agricultural labourers do perform different agricultural activities which do not require specific skill. Women labourers are not trained and unskilled or semi-skilled. Duties they perform is purely dependent on pure observation. They learn this type of work from their family members or parents.
4. Women agricultural labourers do move out but the reason of their moving out is not economical, it is more social based. They do not move out for getting employment. Their migration is in the same district or in the same state.

5. There is a lack of specialisation in the female agricultural labourers. They do not perform same kind of work in the farm. Sometimes they cultivate, they feed and sometimes they do the job of transportation.
6. If caste-wise analysis of female agricultural labour is undergone it can be observed that most of the female agricultural labourers come from backward castes. They are Harijans, Ahir, Rajput, etc. Size of family of the female labourers of this castes is big comparatively. Their living standard is low, income is low but earning members in the family are more.
7. Female agricultural labourers are unorganised. They do not have any national, state or regional level organisation or union. Thus, female labourers of organised sectors do get some more benefits than that of unorganised one. Workers from organised sectors with their united power and collective efforts gets more liberal payment and works under better conditions. Because of unorganised working force female agricultural labourers do not get any of these benefits.
8. Female agricultural labourers are on daily wages. There are permanent labourers in agricultural sector but most of them are males. They work on yearly contract system. But most of the female labourers in this sector are casual and work on daily wages system.
9. Demand of female agricultural labourers is different in different season. When crop is ready for cultivation, demand of female workers increases. But at the time of farming demand declines. Thus, demand differs from season to season.
10. Demand of female agricultural labourers depends on the size of area under cultivation in farm. If farming area is small then demand for female labourers is not present because in most of these types of farm the family members of farmer works. They do not require agricultural labourers. But when farm is large and there are several crops under cultivation demand of agricultural labourers, including female labourerers increases.
11. Demand of female agricultural labour also depends on type or nature of farming activity. If an activity requires more physical strength than demand for male workers is more. In this kind of work male workers are preferred.
12. Employment and wage rate of female agricultural labourers are unstable. If monsoon is good female agricultural labourers increase and they get good wages rate. But in case of drought or flood employment. opportunities for female agricultural labourers declines.

3. PROBLEMS OF FEMALE AGRICULTURAL LABOURERS

Problems of female agricultural labourers are different and specific. Their position is very bad in comparison to other female workers in organised sector. Not only that female agricultural labourers face more problems than that of other unorganised sector labourers. They do get comparatively less employment and wages than organised sectors' female labour. They have to work hard but they are not being paid well. They have serious problems and specific difficulties than male labour. Some of the major problems of female labourers are :

1. There are inadequate employment opportunities for female agricultural labourers. They get seasonal employment. They do not get employment in all days of a season. They do not get work except seasonal days. Number of small farmers is very high in the country, who fullfills their requirement through involving family members in laborious job. Male workers do get more employment than female labour. According to Second Agricultural Labour Research Committee Report male workers got employment for 197 days and worked for 40 days in their own farm. But, female got work for 168 days, were unemployed for about 197 days, whereas male worked for 237 days. In 1964-65, agricultural labour got work for 277 days which declined to 250 days in 1974-75. Female agricultural labour has to remain unemployed for more than six months in a year.
2. Female agricultural labour are less paid. If wage rates are high and number of employment days are low they should not be affected economically, but situation is reverse. They have to work at very low wage rate. For the same kind and type of work female workers are paid less compared to male workers. This difference is marginal. But in a work, which requires greater skill women workers are not paid well as male workers are being paid. At the same time demand for women agricultural labourers is low.
3. Productivity of female agricultural labour is low. It is also very low in agricultural sector. At the price level of 1980-81, in 1950-51 productivity per labour was Rs. 2305 which increased to Rs. 2794 and further increased to Rs. 3157 in 1990. Thus, productivity has not doubled in last 40 years in agricultural sector. Whereas in mining and mineral sector productivity per labour is Rs. 13417, manufacturing sector Rs. 11099, Power Gas and Water supply sector Rs. 14608, construction sector Rs. 16210, commerce and business Rs. 13136 and in other services sector it is 14625. Thus, productivity of agricultural labour is very low compared to other sectors. It is also observed that

productivity of female agricultural labour is very low as compared to that of male labour.

4. Health standard of female agricultural labourers is weak. They have to perform different types of duty at home, in family and in farm. This affects their health and which deteriorates their health. They do not get nutrition food and proper medical attention in case of illness. After delivery they do not have proper time for rest which affects their overall health.
5. Most of the female agricultural labourers lives below poverty line. Their standard of living is also very low. They do not get adequate employment. They are not being paid good wages. Thus, their income is very low. They are not able to satisfy their basic necessities and are not able to get nutrition food.
6. Female agricultural labourers has to work for more hours. They have to work for more than eight hours. In season, they have to work for 10 to 12 hours a day. They work in open. They have to work in heat, rain and cold. This difficult season affects adversely to their health which affects to their daily life.
7. There are chances of accidents in farming works. Condition of work in agricultural sector is very difficult. Female has to work in open, in rain, in heat or in cold. Sometimes equipment of farming can also bring injuries to them. Female agricultural labourers has to work in adverse conditions. Sometimes they are affected by fatigue.
8. Female agricultural labourers are exploited accoding to the definition of exploitation in economics. They are being paid less wage than marginal productivity. They have to work more at low wage rate. Triabal and schedule caste female labourers are more exploited.
9. Female agricultural labourers have to work from early in the morning to late night, continuously. In addition to farming they have to work at home. They have to take care of children, animal husbandary, social gatherings and so on. This working condition adversely affects the health of the labour and her daily life.
10. At the place of female agricultural labourers work, some specific facility like separate sanitation, place of leisure and rest, etc. is desired which is not provided by the farmers.
11. Female agricultural labour do not enjoy their maternity. They do not get proper rest after child birth. Wages for number of days they work are not paid so the worker will not ask for leave in any situation. They also not get proper food after the delivery. In Gujarat state, from 1986-87, scheme for economic assistance is provided to female agricultural labourers before and after the delivery. According to this scheme female labourer

is being paid at minimum wage rate for six weeks after delivery for the first time and for second time she is paid for 4 weeks. The benefits of this scheme do not reach to the female agricultural labourers.

12. Female agricultural labourers do suffer from many social and family problems. Situation of a widow labour, sometimes is very serious. They have to work for most the life but their social status is still not considered to be very high.

After going through all these details, it is observed that problems and difficulties of female agricultural labourers are different, serious and specific. Their problems are not only economic related but also they suffer from social and family problems. Their condition is pity. Government should pay more attention to the problems of female agricultural labourers.

REFERENCES

1. Ahuja, Kanta, "Women Workers in Rural Rajasthan", The A.C.M. State Institute of Public Administration, Jaipur, 1979, p. 81.
2. Government of India, "Economic and Social Status of Women Worker in India", *Labour Bureau*, Ministry of Labour, 1973, p. 7.
3. Hirway, Indira, "A Note on Employment Problem of Rural Women in Gujarat" (ed.), Lakadwala, D.T., *Gujarat Economy*, S.P.I.E.R., 1979, p. 159.
4. *Ibid.*
5. Ahuja, Kanta, "Women Workers in Rural Rajasthan", *op. cit.*, p. 57.
6. Mirulad, V.A., "The Impact of Female Employment on Household Management" (ed.), Jones G.W. "Women in the Urban and Industrial Workforce, South East and East Asia", Australian National University, 1948, p. 385.
7. Government of India, "Economic and Social Status of Women Worker in India", *op. cit.*, p. 27.
8. International Labour Organisation, "Equal Value", Report VI, 33rd Session, Geneva, 1949, pp. 98-99.
9. Government of Bombay, "Report of the Textile Enquiry Committee", Vol. II, Final Report, 1940, p. 80.
10. Government of Bombay, "Report of the Committee on Employment in Road Construction and Building Operation", Bombay, 1957, p. 7.
11. Award of the Industrial Tribunal on the Conditions of Labour in the Textile Industry in Madras Presidency, 1947, p. 30.

11

Trade Union Activity in India

"Equal cadre people get limited to achieve their same goal."

—G.D.H. Cole

Outline of the Chapter

1. Introduction.
2. Stages of the Trade Union Movement in India.
3. Overall Observation after Independence.
4. Central large Trade Organisations.
5. Conclusion

1. INTRODUCTION

Trade union is an important part of labour movement. So, trade union activity can be known as labour movement. Prof. Cole describes labour movement as an activity which reflects a particular social condition. Equal cadre people get united to achieve their same goal.[1] The wage earners unitedly join this activity to improve their condition immediately or in near future.[2]

Labour movement and trade union activity are almost identical, but there is slight difference between them. Labour movement is a movement for labourers, while trade union activity is being conducted by labourers.

According to Labour Commission reports, "The main elements in the development of trade unions of workers in every country have been more or less the same."[3]

2. STAGES OF TRADE UNION MOVEMENT IN INDIA

In India trade union activity started long before independence. Its development is not continuous but it has developed stage-wise. Its various stages have been represented variously by many experts.

Duffy N.F. in his well known book *Industrial Relations in India* describes trade union activity in following stages :

1. Stage before 1920.
2. Civil war stage between 1920 to 1939.
3. Second World War stage between 1939 to 1946.
4. Post-Independence stage of 1947 to 1962.

C.B. Kumar in his book. "Development of Industrial Relations in India" (1961; p. 5) divides trade union activities in four stages :

1. Initial Stage *i.e.*, 1875 to 1918.
2. Civil War Stage *i.e.*, 1928 to 1938.
3. Second World War Stage *i.e.*, 1939 to 1945.
4. Post-war Stage *i.e.*, 1946 to 1958.

Dr. Memoriya has divided trade union activity in five stages in his book "Dynamics of Industrial Relations in India".

1. State between 1875 to 1918

The problems of exploitation started with industrialisation with industrial development. Government started some welfare schemes to solve labour problems.[4] In this period Indian labourers were in worse condition compared to British labourers.[5] During that time efforts were not made to solve their problems by collective bargaining.[6]

Because, they came from rural area and they were not united.[7]

In 1875 Sorabji Bengalji and in 1884 N.M. Lokhande tried to draw attention towards grave and serious condition of labourers. British Government was not interested in labour welfare but just to get Indian products cheaper it showed interest that women and children may not work in industry. In 1881, Indian Factories Act was formed which was amended in 1891 and 1911. In this Act working hours were reduced and condition of workers and children working in industry was improved.

Some events like second Bombay Factory Commission in 1884, inquiry of Mr. John, Large gathering of workers on 21st April 1890, memorandum to the Government, gathering of 17,000 workers invited trade union activity in India.[8]

In 1890 Bombay Mill-hands Association was started by Shri N.M. Lokhande. This was the first Indian Association. The owners agreed for one weekly holiday. This is the first labour union formed by Mr. Lokhande. This association had published a newspaper named "Dinbandhu". During this spell other unions were also formed, like Printers Unions of Calcutta — 1905, Bombay Postal Union, Bombay and Madras — 1907, Kamdar Hitwardhan Sabha — 1909, Social Service

League — 1910. The Institutes like Satya Sodhak Sabha, Maharastra, Theosophical Society — Madras, Brahmo Samaj — Calcutta etc. Also bust up labour movement.

The main aims of labour organisation were to solve labour problems, constitutionally and conduct welfare-oriented activity.

These labour associations drew peoples attention towards labourers, problems and their working condition. Foundation of Trade Unions was laid after First World War. By that time Owners Associations too came in existence to safeguard their interest. These unions were Mumbai and Bengal Chamber of Commerce, Bombay Mill Owners Association — Calcutta Traders Association, British Indian Association, Indian Chamber of Commerce etc. during 1869 to 1881. These unions adopted strong attitude towards strike, tried to protect their profits and tried to increase their return on capital.

Death of two founders gave shock to trade union activity.[9] Yet it continued upto 1st decade of 20th century. V.V. Giri quotes that, "Trade Unions played remarkable role between 1904 to 1911". During this period Bombay Mill strikes, Railway strikes and Government Press strikes took place. In 1908 in Mumbai Labour movement was in peak due to constant six days political party increased political party support in strike.[10] This strike increased political awareness of labourers.

The political factors supported labour movement but that activity developed very slowly, due to inefficiency of labourers and weakness of trade unions. Upto 1918 trade union activity was going on according to constitutional methods. In which systems like memorandum, legal action committees were being adopted.[11] Majority of unions were unstable, very light actions were taken, there was very little knowledge of collective bargaining and permanent registration of trade unions.[12] Shri Dutt notes regarding Bombay Millshand Association that, "The association has no existence as an organised body, having no role of membership, no funds, nor rule..."[13]

During that time the intellectuals, activists and politicians had leaded trade unions.[14]

The factors like pains of workers, initial failure in unity etc., also effected trade union activity.

2. Stage between 1918 to 1924

The year 1918 was memorable for trade union activity. Because from this year a new era of development started. Command of trade unions were handed over to the hands of social workers from the hands of politicians. Permanent roots of trade unions were implanted in Indian soil.[15] During this period industrial unrest increased, troubles were also increased and it became necessary to take collective steps, as demand of increase in wage became stronger due to increase in living expense.[16] During these spell freedom activity became stronger, awareness of workers increased and demand for equality with British owner were also became stronger. This awareness gave inspiration for new zeal and ideals.[17] Many Indian soldiers joined in labour force. Status of workers went high due to establishment. of I.L.O. (International Labour Organisation). All these factors gave new opportunity to trade unions.[18]

During this period some new trade unions were formed like Indian Seamen Union, in Calcutta and Mumbai, Punjab Press Employees' Association, Railway Works Union, Bombay, M.S.M. Railway Men's Union, Madras, Madras Textile Labour Union, The Postmen and Port Trust Employees Union, Bombay and Calcutta, Jamshedpur Labour Association.

Madras Textile Union formed by B.P. Vadiya in 1918 can be called first union of modern style. They have sanctioned one hour's rest from owners. They have started taking steps for their development by starting co-operative society and library for their members.[19] Seventeen new trade unions had been formed between the end of 1917 to the end of 1919.[20] By the inspiration of Mahatma Gandhi Spinners' Union and Weavers' Union were being formed in Ahmedabad in 1920. Similarly, Textile Labour Association was formed too.

On 30th October in 1920 representatives of 64 Trade Unions met who were representing 1,40,854 labourers and All India Trade Union Congress was being formed under the chairmanship of Lala Lajpatrai. This large organisation was supported by national leaders. By the formation of this large labour organisation, co-ordination in labourers work became easy and they were being inspired for developing labourers' interest and to mobilise the Indian labourers' economically, socially and politically and to participate the labour force in freedom movement. At that time 125 Trade Unions and 2.5 lakh members were attached with AITUC.[21]

During the period of Civil War Trade Union movement was effected. Demand for labourers' right increased. Increase in Industrial strikes were noticed and for the first time management for the solution of industrial unrest (problems) was being considered.[22]

After 1919 trade union activity became widespread for this. Dr. V.V. Giri notes that till the end of 1925 number of trade unions increased four times and its number of members increased much higher. In real sense labour movement became united and sense of co-operation increased among labour class.[23]

Royal Commission on Labour has noted that, "Labour awareness in India was also developed with world. The labourers started demanding for wage, working hours and other demands. The labour activity affected national politics also."[24]

This movement developed well but it did not succeed in textile industries. It progressed in Railway, P & T, Shipping, Engineering and Telecommunication Sector, it did not developed in sectors like Mines, Jute industries and Textile industries.[25]

3. Stage between 1924 to 1934

Due to long duration strikes industrial unrest increased in 1924 and labour unions were sentenced to jail. At that time AITUC was leading labour class. In 1927, 57 unions joined it, with 1,50,555 members. Labour movement went forward due to factors like abate in real wage, national movement and arrest of freedom fighters.

In 1926-27, numbers of labourers and farmers increased. And their local units formed "Akhil Bhartiya Shramik and Kisan Party". With the formation of this party importance of rightist wing and rightist factors in trade union movement increased. Numbers of strikes increased. In 1928, 316 lakhs human days were lost due to strikes. Importance of communist factors increased in trade unions and in Mumbai they have formed "Girani Kamgar Union", Similarly, G.I.P. Railway Mens' Union was formed. Both these labour union members were 54,000 and 45,000 respectively. In this way communist factors entered trade unions in main centres *viz.*, Mumbai, Ahmedabad, Delhi, Calcutta etc. Effect of communist factors was such a high that government was also impressed.

The rightist and the leftist these two trends began to lead trade unions according to their own ideology, that is the peculiarity of labour movement. Besides that, the Geneva Group and Moscow Group also started affecting labour movement. These two, rightist and leftist, factors tried to attract AITUC with their world level organisation at international stage. So disputes between these two groups began to grow.

Some disputable matters occurred, due to these factors. So 24 recognized unions separated from AITUC. They declared that interest of labour class is jeopardized, due to control and leadership of new majority in administrative council. They established "The All India Trade Union Federation". Hence, number of AITUC trade union was reduced to 21 from 51. And number of members remained 94,000 from 9 lakhs. This large trade union tried to concentrate on constructive activity. In 1930, 104 labour unions were registered with 2.42 lakh members.

In 1931, Calcutta, Summit differences on basic matters between leftist wing and communists, emerged and there was one more split in AITUC. Shri B.D. Randive and Shri S.B. Deshpande formed a new union named "Red Trade Union Congress (R.T.U.C.): Thus, these three trade unions *i.e.* AITUC, AITUF and RTUC began to work.

4. 1935-1938 Spell

The spell between 1924-1934, was spell of splitting due to conflict between the right wing and the left. While spell between 1935-1938 was the spell of consolidation between trade unions.

The efforts of consolidation done by Royal group and leaders of all India Railwaymen federation seemed to be fruitfull. Railwaymen Federation had formed a committee for it, in their 1932. summit. This committee proposed all labour unions, to come on one stage to achieve same goals. It found out some common standards which were agreeable to AITUF and INTUC; in 1933, National Federation of Labour (NFL) was formed in New Delhi for the unity of labour organisations. AITUF and Railway union was merged in National Trade Union Federation. However, AITUC and RTUC remained away from it.

Price of labour union spliting was very severe. In 1933, more than 50,000 workers were retrached one-sidedly in Mumbai only. Wages were reduced in all mills of Mumbai. Labour movement was obstructed. Moral was dispersed and its quality deteriorated.[26] In this condition unity of workers and their union became inevitable In 1935, RTUC decided to join AITUC. In 1937 general election, Indian National Congress gave importance to workers and their unions and promised to solve their problems. Congress came in power in seven states. In 1937 there were 379 strikes, in which 6.47 lakhs people had joined and 8982 lakhs human days were lost. In 1936-37 there were 271 labour unions which went upto 562 in 1938-39 and number of members raised upto 3.99 lakhs from 2.61 lakhs.[27]

In 1938, consolidation efforts of shri V.V. Giri succeeded and NTUF merged in AITUC.[28] Thus, once again AITUC became large trade union.

5. 1939-1945 Spell

Second World War started in 1945. Main two ideologies were prevailing among AITUC leaders and labour leaders ; regarding giving support to world war. One side thought that world war is against fascist factors and hence it must be supported. While others believed that it is concerned with Britain and India has nothing to do with it. So they prefered to remain away from it. Due to this reason, once again there was a split in AITUC in 1941. 200 unions with 3,00,000 members formed **Indian Federation of Labour.** In 1942, government approved it as representative of labour class. This union demanded for minimum wages in return of supporting war keeping up moral of labourers and partnership in production plans according to war needs. Government provided fund for it. In 1942 number of labour unions reached up to 222 and number of members reached upto 4,07,737 in 1944.

In 1942 "Quit India" movement became stronger, congressmen and the socialists were arrested and command of AITUC, was taken by communists.

Government and owners took some labour welfare steps during war. Labour Unions were being approved and strikes and lockouts were banned. The owners and the workers started understanding each other. Triside Summit met in 1942. In 1944-45 number of labour unions were 865 and members were increased to 8.89 lakhs. So AITUC became stronger than IFL. All these factors boost up trade union activities. These numbers deereased to 601 and 8 lakhs respectively in 1947.

6. Post-Independence Stage

When efforts to recognize AITUC failed, the people who did not believe in its ideology, they seperated from it and established Indian National Trade Union Congress (INTUC) in 1947.

On 3rd and 4th May 1947, a meeting was held by Hind Majdur Seva Sangh in New Delhi, in which an agenda was passed to form National Central Organisation.

On 25th September 1947, Congress requested their members to join INTUC with their unions and members. On 20th January 1948 Sardar Patel also appealed for the same.

Ahmedahad Textile Labour Association (ATLA) has done remarkable help to INTUC and has provided guidance and leadership. At that time there were 200 labour unions and 57,500 members were attached to INTUC. It developed rapidly and became largest trade union of labourers and labour unions. Position of AITUC was replaced by INTUC. INTUC became Congress ideology.

In 1948, socialist leaders seperated from Congress and established "Praja Samajvadi Party". Socialists of INTUC also seperated from it and made a new central union named "Hindustan Majdoor Panchayat". This federation and Indian Federation of Labour both together formed "Hind Mazdoor Sabha" (H.M.S.). The leftist viewers were not satisfied with this union. They formed "United Trade Union Congress" (UTUC) in 1949 and they supported communist ideology.

Thus, 4 large unions *viz.*, Congress sided INTUC Socialist party sided H.M.S., Communist sided AITUC and Revolutionary Socialist party sided U.T.U.C. came in existence.

After 1952, efforts for unification of trade unions were made. The joint meeting of AITUC and UTUC in 1953 failed. In 1956, many unions shown trust in joint movement and joint programme. INTUC and HMS made some code of conduct to achieve co-operation. HMS requested central unions to unite on common principles.

In 1958, HMS and UTUC decided to give combined fight to AITUC. In 1959 some socialist party labour leaders seperated from HMS and formed "Hind Mazdoor Panchayat". In 1962, confederation of free trade union was established with the support of Swatantra Party and International Confederation of Christian Trade Unions.

During the war with China INTUC, HMS and AITUC were alleged of anti-national and anti-social trends.

In 1970, with the split of communist party leadership of AITUC was taken by CPI. Whereas CPM established centre of Indian Trade Union. Similarly, division of Congress in 1972, directly effected INTUC. The leaders of "Sanstha Congress" seperated from INTUC and established National Labour Organisation (NLO).

In 29th session of standing labour committee held on 23rd and 24th July 1970, 27th session of Indian Labour Organisation held on October 22nd and 23rd, 1971 and in various meetings of central labour unions, partial accord was done. It was decided that, if there are more than one union in any factory, in that condition secret voting may be conducted and the members of the union who gets majority shall be recognised union. Following this stage National Council of Central Trade Unions (NCCTV) was established which was representing AITUC, INTUC and HMS. Thus, Central Labour Union leaders came on stage. In September 1972, its rival organisation *i.e.* United Council of Trade Union (UCTU) was formed.

By general observation, it can be seen that in 1947 registered unions were 2,766, became 33,023 in 1979, while number of members reached upto 46.61 lakhs from 16.63 lakhs.

3. OVERALL OBSERVATION AFTER INDEPENDENCE

In 1951-52 there were 118 owners unions with 8,000 members which became 758 and 18,000 accordingly in 1984.

During this period number of registered labour unions reached upto 43,309 from 4,505 and number of members became 64.14 lakhs from 19.88 lakhs. In 1985 there were total 45,067 trade unions from which

7,815 unions were filing returns. Their strength of members was 64.33 lakhs and average number of members per union was 823.[29]

In 1985, there were 338 unions with 4.53 lakh members, which were attached with agro-oriented activities. There were 133 unions with 2.10 lakhs members in mines and mineral sector. In manufacturing sector there were 3,304 trade unions and 18.36 lakhs members. There were 2.58 lakh members of 155 unions in electricity, gas and water supply sector. In construction field there were 236 unions with 1.08 lakh members. There were 464 unions with 1.26 lakh members in lodging, boarding and hotel industries. There were 830 labour unions with 17.69 lakh members in transport, communication and storage sector. All these unions were sending report. Similarly 616 unions with 4.69 lakh members of finance sector, insurance sector etc. 1,021 unions of social service and personal service sector and other 777 unions with 8.55 lakh members of other sectors were received from total 7,815 labour unions.[30]

Thus, after independence various labour unions have been established according to different political views. Every party has their own labour wings, which act as their mouthpiece. These unions, also split with the split in relevant political party.

After independence, labour unions have clearly effected Industrial policy, labour policy and labour laws.

For effective and skilled function for solving labour problems it is needed that labour union should remain away from political parties.

The trade union activity was effected during emergency. In post-emergency general election Janta Party government of oppositions came in power. So, with the unification of opposite labour unions their leaders got opportunity to come on one platform. But before that process starts, Janta Party was thrown away from power.

And after shorter term government of late shri Charan Singh as a result of election Congress (I) came to power. So, importance of INTUC increased once again.

When late Shri Rajiv Gandhi started modernisation and modern technology labour leaders expressed their fear that this would boost up unemployment.

From 1991, Indian Government has adopted new economic policy, modernisation, privatisation and foreign collaboration, all labour unions except INTUC are opposing it. To express the protest they called for two nation-wide strikes. The second strike was on 16th June 1992. Similarly, these labour unions strongly opposed government policy of shut down the sick units. But government has given frequent assurance that it would not take any step which is harmful to labourers. Labour Unions observed nation-wide strike in December, 1998 for opposing new economic reforms.

4. CENTRAL LARGE TRADE ORGANISATION

The State Trade Unions are working as per guideline of central level trade unions. As it has been discussed above these central trade unions are attached with different political parties. Now, let us make detailed study of main national level trade unions.

1. The Indian National Trade Union Congress (INTUC). On November 17th, 1948, Hind Majdoor Sevak Sangh which was guided by some Gandhian Congressmen passed a resolution to form a trade union of national cadre. On 4th May 1949, INTUC was established. Congress formed a new union, because AITUC was highly influenced by the communists. At that time Sardar Patel told that it is not possible to improve AITUC, it registers bogus members. So INTUC was started under the leadership of S.C. Banerji.

Some important motives of INTUC were decided and an appeal was made to fulfil these motives. These motives are as under :

1. Formation of uniform social system in which all its members get advantages of development. To avoid exploitation and inequality to develop human approach and to avoid centralisation of any anti-social system.
2. Keeping due control over industries to provide them status of national property.
3. To increase labour co-operation in industrial management.
4. Formation of total employment-oriented system, for best utilisation of human power.
5. To satisfy social, political and civil interests of workers.
6. Establishment of judicious industrial relation.
7. Disposal of industrial disputes without stopping the work by discussions and commitments or by judiciary if required.
8. To take legal steps like "strike" or "satyagraha" if disputes are not solved by legal system or judiciary.
9. Quick disposal of strikes by peaceful and effective steps.
10. To develop sense of dedication, service, co-operation and mutual help assistance among workers.
11. To develop sense of responsibility towards society and industry in workers.
12. To develop standard of discipline and efficiency among workers.

All these aims, reflect philosophy of peace, discipline, dedication non-violence and Gandhian truth. This union recommends peaceful way of negotiations and to go on strike only in unavoidable circumstances.

Since 1949, INTUC is attached with International Labour Organisation; besides that it is founder member of "The International Confederation of Free Trade Union Congress" (ICFTC). INTUC publishes two weeklies, "Indian Worker" in English and "Mazdoor Sandesh" in Hindi.

2. All India Trade Union Congress (AITUC). As per resolution passed by united workers, Mumbai and with the efforts of delegates of the 30th October 1920, summit AITUC was established. In this summit national leaders like Motilal Nehru, Sardar Patel, Anne Beasant remained present. Wedgewood from British trade union congress also remained present. Lala Lajpatrai was elected as its first president.

Aims (Objectives) of AITUC was as under :

1. Establishment of socialist state in India.
2. Nationalisation and socialization of tools of production and distribution.
3. To upgrade economic and social condition of workers soon.
4. To look after and protect needs, rights and interest of all workers.
5. To work for freedom of speech, freedom of union, make freedom of press and to get right of work for labourers.
6. Consolidation of functions of all trade unions, who are attached with AITUC.
7. To remove political or economic (financial) benefits on the basis of caste, creed, community, religion etc.
8. To obtain and maintain right of strike.

Above matters show that this union is highly influenced by the communist effect. In it, hard actions like strikes are preferred to peaceful ways. Procedure of AITUC seems to be influenced by theory and guideline of Karl Marx. In the states with Marxist theories like Kerala, West Bengal and Tripura, hold of this union is very strong. Over and above that, it works efficiently in main industrial houses. It is attached with world federation of trade union. It publishes magazine named "Vishva-darshan".

3. Hind Mazdoor Sabha and Hind Mazdoor Panchayat *i.e.*, HMS and HMP. When the socialists separated from Congress, they were neither interested nor they had faith (trust) in Congress guided INTUC or Communist managed AITUC. So, they started a new nation-wide labour union named "Hind Mazdoor Panchayat". In 1949 it merged with Indian Federation of Labour and came in existence as "Hind Mazdoor Sabha". This is a basic unit of "Praja Samajvadi Party".

The leaders who were not satisfied with "Hind Mazdoor Sabha", they separated from it in 1962 and established "Hind Mazdoor Panchayat". There is no major difference in thinkings of these two unions. They separated only due to disputes among their national leaders. The aims of both these unions are as following :

1. Establishment of Democratic Socialist Society in India and to enhance social, political and economic interests of workers.
2. To provide total opportunities to workers for their physical and mental development.
3. To avail living wage to all workers.
4. To give assurance of work to all workers.
5. To provide availability of social security and intensive like medical facility by the industries to the workers.
6. To make efforts for due rest for workers by means of proper working hours and leave with pay.
7. To provide sufficient housing facility.
8. To arrange for free and mandatory education and vocational guidance.
9. To get recognization for right of collective bargaining.
10. To co-operate with national and international unions who have equal goals and targets.
11. To achieve and maintain liberty of gathering, meeting, speech, press and strike.

For overall development of workers, it has same thoughts like INTUC. But INTUC believes in hard steps, while it believes in negotiations and peaceful steps. That is the main difference between them. Though it is influenced by Marxist Ideology, it has democratic and calm approach and use strikes as final tool.

4. United Trade Union Congress (UTUC). On 27th December, 1948 unsatisfied leaders of the Hind Mazdoor Sabha met in Calcutta and decided to call for a meeting of labour leaders. United Trade Union Committee was made. It arranged a labour leaders meeting on 13th April, 1949 in which a new union named United Trade Union Congress (UTUC) was formed.

Effort was made that this union remains pure labour union which is away from political parties and works only for their workers. Yet, there was hold of basic leftist leaders on it. Main aims of UTUC were as under :

1. Formation of socialist society in nation.
2. Foundation of labourer's and farmer's rule in India.

3. Nationalization and socialization of production, distribution and exchange.
4. To safeguard and preserve cultural, political, social and financial interest of labourers.
5. To Obtain unity and co-ordination in Labour Movement.

It seems from these aims that they are identical with AITUC aims; because their leaders were in AITUC previously. This union prefers peaceful steps like agreements, accord meeting etc. and takes hard steps like strikes as a ultimate tool.

5. Bhartiya Mazdoor Sangh (BMS). On July 23rd 1954, Jan Sangh established this union in their Bhopal summit. Most of the Jan Sangh leaders had joined Janta Government and afterwards they formed Bhartiya Janta Party. After fall of Janta Government they seperated from it. This union has clear effect of them.

Aims of this union are as under :

1. Formation of casteless society, in which full employment can be achieved and foundation of monetary democracy in which aim of service can be obtained instead of aim of profit.
2. Formation of industrial social system in which every person attached with industry acts as a partner of industry.
3. To help workers in forming unions which work the service of motherland.
4. To preserve right to go on strike.
5. To develop thoughts of integrity, dedication and co-operation.
6. To create sense of responsibility and equality towards industry and society in labourers.

It seems from these aims that this is a non-political union which is production-oriented and gives top priority to nationalism and Indian culture. It believes to make labourers nationalist, labour-oriented industry and industrial nation.

This union protests against state interference and emphasis on self-discipline and moral responsibility. It gives respect to customer as a third factor. It emphasises on patriotism in labourers dedication and self-responsibility.

6. National Front of Indian Trade Unions (NFITU). This union was established in 1967. It claims that it concentrates only on labour functions, remaining away from politics, political parties or hold of owner or government. Considering the relations between labour unions and industries following aims are kept by union :

1. To liberate labour unions from hold or influence of government or industrialists and to co-ordinate them.

2. To make workers committed towards national dedication, protection and defence.
3. To aware workers towards their duties and responsibilities, besides their right.
4. To provide all facilities to their members for recognization and create effective leadership for their right.
5. To provide assurance for smooth life to workers and improvement in their social status.
6. To help labour movement for rise in real wage.
7. Implementation and formation of laws for the welfare of the members of the valid unions and to protect right and interest of labour class.

Above aims show that this union has full faith only in labourers and their union activities. It wishes to work for labourers and trade unions, remaining away from influence of industrialists, politics or government.

In 4th congress of this union in November 1975, agenda has been announced that every human have basic rights. This union has respect towards Indian Constitution, ideals of UNO and documents of International Labour Organisation. If studies for preservation and protection of moral interests, physical interest and cultural interests of Indian workers. Its function is independent and free from religious, political or government pressure. It accepts private sector with public control. It tries for uplifting status of workers. It also tries to awake workers for change in society.

7. Centre of Indian Trade Union (CITU). Some communist leaders who seperated from AITUC in 1970, they started this union. Its fundamental aims which were decided are as under :

1. It is essential to establish socialist society, to stop exploitation of labour class. This can be done by socialization of production tools, distribution and exchange.
2. This union fights and shall keep fighting for liberty, financial and social rights of workers including right of strike.
3. It recommends immediate nationalisation of monopolised foreign unit, which exploit workers. It also demands for nationalisation of large monopolised units which collect high price from customer and make large profit at the cost of workers.
4. This union shall fight against anti-democratic elements anti-union elements and anti-public policies of government. It shall also oppose the policies, which impose tax and heavy price hike on workers and common mass and the policy which protects the capitalists and zamindars *i.e.*, landlords, social reformation is not possible without class-war.

Thus, CITU is a hard core union which believes that government pampers the capitalists. Exploitation, inequality and labour problems are due to government policies. So due to this belief it appeals for protesting and fighting against government policies. It believes that war between classes is essential to avoid exploitation from the capitalists.

5. CONCLUSION

Though there are many national trade unions among them INTUC, AITUC, HMS and UTUC are main and important four trade unions. The aims and management of these four unions are identical but their working pattern is different. These unions are attached with one or another international union. These unions are attached with political parties also.

The Indian labour movement is not pure. It is mixed up with politics. Nowadays majority of workers are not united. Their condition is pitiable, particularly the condition of casual workers, child workers and female workers is very miserable.

REFERENCES

1. Cole. G.D.H., *A Sharp History of British Working Class Movement*, London, pp. 11-12.
2. Commons, J.R., *Labour Movement Encyclopeadia of Social Services*, New York, 1939, p. 69.5.
3. National Commission on Labour Report, 1969, p. 227.
4. Clow, A.C., *The State and Industry*, 1928, p. 137.
5. Buchanan, D.H., *The Development of Capitalistic Enterprise in India*, 1934, p. 300.
6. Report of the Royal Com. on Labour, 1931.
7. Quoted by Punekar, S.D., in *Trade Unionism in India*, 1948.
8. Giri V.V., *Labour Problems in Indian Industries*, 1972, p. 2.
9. Mathur, J.S. and A.S. Mathur, *The Trade Union Movement in India*, 1957, p. 38.
10. Gurtu, Sachirani, *Jagjiwan Ram on Labour Problems*, p. 38.
11. Sharma, G.K., *Labour Movement in India*, 1963, p. 69.
12. Gurtu, Sachirani, *op. cit.*, p. 38.
13. Dutt, Rajni Palm, *India Today*, 1949, p. 375.
14. Crouch, Harold, *Trade Unions and Politics in India*, 1966, p. 58.
15. Giri, V.V., *op. cit.*, p. 90.
16. Labour Gazett, Bombay, IInd, s, p. 10.
17. J. Nehru, *Towards Freedom*, 1941, p. 75.
18. Crouch, Harold, *op. cit.*, p. 59.
19. Shiva Rao, B., *Industrial Worker in India*, 1939, p. 13.
20. Joshi, N.M., *Trade Unionism in India*, p. 9.
21. Quoted by N.K. Bosh (ed.), *Selection from Gandhi*, 1948, pp. 133-134.
22. Kumar, C.B., *op. cit.*, pp. 91-92.
23. Giri. V.V., *op. cit.*, p. 13.
24. Report of the Royal Commission on Labour, p. 13.

25. Loknathan, P.S., *Industrial Welfare in India,* Report of the Royal Commission on Labour, pp. 317 and 319.
26. Brecher, Michel, *Nehru : A Political Biography*, 1939, p. 141.
27. Karnik, V.B., *Indian Trade Unions : A Survey*, 1960, p. 89.
28. Punekar, S.D., *op. cit.*, pp. 332-334.
29. *Indian Labour Statistics*, 1985.
30. *Indian Labour Year Book*, 1985.

12

Unemployment

"The difference between total employment and real employment is unemployment."

—*Encyclopaedia Britanica*

Outline of the Chapter

1. Introduction.
2. Meaning and Definition of unemployment.
3. Main Approaches.
4. Forms of Unemployment.
5. Magnitude of the Problem.
6. Measurement of Unemployment.
7. Estimates of Unemployment.
8. New Economic Policy, Labour Market and its Problems.

1. INTRODUCTION

Unemployment is a serious problem for underdeveloped nation like India. Of course in developed nations also unemployment prevails. But in those nations unemployed people are being protected by social security schemes. But in underdeveloped nations unemployment and underemployment leads to poverty.

In India, steps to increase employment have been taken in planning. But percentage of unemployment has increased. Today problem of unemployment is very grave, even though government has paid special attention towards eradication of unemployment. Some labour leaders and experts believe that new economic and industrial policy shall worsen the problem of unemployment. Government has decided to shut down sick public units. So, it is apparent that their workers shall be unemployed. But government has assured that government shall think of workers, while closing such units. A special strategy has been planned out in 8th programme and has been set up as a part of full employment.

2. MEANING AND DEFINITION OF UNEMPLOYMENT

Lack of employment is unemployment. And employment is the condition in which compensation is received either in cash or kind; in return of personal direct and active partnership in production process[1], lack of such beneficial employment is unemployment.

1. According to Mrs. John Robinsion, "In irregular or private sector many a times production tools seems to be inactive, where the workers are sacked and land remains uncultivated."[2] Here, we have to consider concept of unemployment in context with workers only and not in context with tools of production.
2. According to Encyclopaedia of Social Sciences, Unemployment is such a situation of the labour market where supply of labour power is more than its opportunity."[3]
3. According to Encyclopaedia Britanica "Unemployment means difference between total employment and real employment."[4]
4. 8th conference of labour statisticians at Geneva in 1954 had defined unemployment. According to that in undermentioned conditions a person is said to be unemployed :
   (i) A person who is available for job, whose job agreement is completed and who is being suspended for a short period and is in search of work for wage or benefit.
   (ii) He is available for work for a stipulated period, who is in search of job, who has not done any work previously and whose status is different to the worker.
   (iii) Jobless people who are available for job at present.
   (iv) Who is jobless due to uncertain or temporary lockout.[5]
5. A Jobless person who is above age group of 15-16 years and in search of Job and is available for the job can be said unemployed.[6]

   A person who is on leave with or without pay due to industrial unrest, sickness, accident etc. is not included in unemployed.[7]
6. On the basis of International Labour Organisation's concept an authorised concept regarding employment and unemployment was given by Central Statistical Organisation.[8] Discontiuation of employment is unemployment.[9]
7. According to Prof. R.C. Saksena, unemployment is a condition, where capable people of working age group want to work, but they do not get the job at current pay scale.[10]

3. MAIN APPROACHES

Various formulas were formed to measure unemployment at various times. In 50's there were only two formulas.[11] First trend was inclined with direct unemployment. Other was attached with labour residual, on the basis of productivity and working skill with reference to worker's selection of work and rest.[12] In overpopulated underdeveloped nations unemployment is measured by this formula.

Rajkrishna divides concept of unemployment measurement in three parts : (1) Time, (2) Income and (3) Desire.[13] A person can be told unemployed or semi-unemployed if he gets job, which is for short work can be called unemployed. A person can be told employed only if he gets income from work from which minimum living standard suggested by Dandekar and Rath can be maintained.

Noble Prize Winner Prof. A.K. Sen puts forward two concepts of measurement of unemployment with reference to income and belief.[14] A person can be known as employed only if his income is connected with job. From production point of view a person is called unemployed if a person living in joint family gets share whether he works or does not work. If production does not decrease by removing an employer then he can be called unemployed with reference to unemployed then he may be called so, by concept of belief.

4. FORMS OF UNEMPLOYMENT

Unemployment which takes place when business or trade does not expand or decrease and demand and supply of labour remains steady is called normal unemployment. Fluctuations can be seen in most of the firms every month or every year in connection of employment. But there is no daily change. Daily changes take place in profession like construction where so many things are to be done at a time and it is not possible to keep permanent workers due to technical reasons. In such trades there shall be large labour residuals which shall lead to unemployment. This is called abnormal unemployment.

Some businesses are seasonal business. In such business there is difference in winter and summer. Agriculture is a seasonal business. Summer is good for construction work, while demand of coal is more in winter. Except these time there prevails unemployment. This is called seasonal unemployment. In such sectors high wages during the season and low wages in off season is observed.

According to Harber and Levinson,[15] there are four main factors for seasonal unemployment : (1) Weather; (2) Traditions; (3) Industrial frame-works in which small units are not capable of adopting modern system; (4) Average income level.

The building, civil and public works committee of international labour organization has studied and made following conclusions on seasonal unemployment[16] :

(i) There was more seasonal unemployment in construction sector during 30th decade compared to 20th decade according to experience of Belgium, Denmark, France, Netherland and Norway; while in Canada, Germany, Poland and America there was less unemployment in 30's compared to 20's.

(ii) Seasonal unemployment decreased during 2nd World War, due to utilization of manpower and materials for purpose of war.

(iii) Seasonal unemployment cannot be eliminated by external task.

(iv) Traditions, low wage rates, lack of work finance availability, size of the units etc. are the other factors effecting seasonal unemployment.

Disguised unemployment is an unemployment in the form of human power wastage. When a person is working but its marginal productivity is zero, it is called disguised unemployment. Production does not decrease even if such person is removed from work. In India large scale disguised unemployment is observed in agriculture, trade, administration, etc. sectors. This is wastage of human power. Energy of such people can be used if the problem of disguised unemployment can be solved by planning of human resources.

Agricultural or rural unemployment is a major problem in India. According to "Royal Commission" report, a farmer remains unemployed. Radhakamal Mukherji Observed that in agriculture sectors of U.P. employment is obtained for 200 days only. Same condition is there in southern India, according to Dr. Slater.

Rural background, joint family system, undue attachment for the land, uncertainty of rain, seasonal cultivation, lack of other jobs, population growth etc. factors are responsible for rural unemployment.

5. MAGNITUDE OF THE PROBLEM

Unemployment is a crucial issue of Indian economy, a society and polities also. There are several employment generation schemes implemented since last many years. But its results are very far from the satisfaction. Therefore, unemployment is to remain burning problem for us. There are various types of unemployment, prevailing in India. First and important nature of unemployment is open unemployment which is referred as a workers capable and willing to be hired as full time workers but are unable to find such work. Open unemployment manifesting itself on a significant scale only in the twentieth century, with the development of a modern factory industrial system in the metropolitan cities and other urban areas. Industrialisation and its nature is responsible for present open unemployment problem. Underemployment defined as a situation where a person willing to work full time defined according to the prevailing standards, but, is unable to find full time work. It can also refers as a underwaged full time work situation also. Disguised unemployment can refers to a situation where there is surplus labour in the reference of marginal physical productivity of a worker is less than the product wage.

As we noted earlier process and nature of industrialisation is responsible for this open unemployment, because it encourages the conversion of open unemployment from underemployment and disguised unemployment. This conversion is occurred because of four factors.[17]

(1) The detachment of workers from land where previously they were occupied as owners or tenants or labourers,

(2) The detachment of members from joint families where total product they were sharing previously as dependents,

(3) Increase of literacy, and

(4) Increase of women's participation in labour force.

Basically employment have three basic components or aspects :

(1) The income component employment gives in income to the employed.

(2) The production aspect, employment yields on output.

(3) The recognition aspect employment gives a person the recognition of being engaged in something worth while.[18]

Employment created output and income. In this context we can say that unemployment is a waste, a loss of potential output and income. Employment gives earned income. Without employment income is a charity or welfare mean derives from social security programmes towards unemployer and poor people. In underdeveloped country like India to maintain the unemployed people is very difficult.

In our country there is co-existence of labour surplus and shortage of essential goods at a time. This is a result of unemployment.

Unemployment problem in different regions of the country shows that it has varied from country to country. In India, unemployment is not due to lack of effective demand like Western industrialists developed countries. Keynesian prescription is not useful to solve the problem of Indian unemployment. There are vast types of unemployment in India. It can refers as an open unemployment, underemployment, frictional and depressional unemployment, seasonal and disguised unemployment, rural and urban unemployment, educated unemployment, agricultural and non-agricultural unemployment.

In rural areas people worked at lower productivity which is result in disguised unemployment. The higher growth of increase of population dependent upon land without a corresponding increase in the area of cultivation has resulted in a surplus population engaged in agriculture.

The committee on unemployment rightly felt that the concept of unemployment as the term is generally understood was not applicable to rural areas and the method of working out period of unemployment was arbitrary.[19] In the rural areas unemployment generally takes the form of underemployment. Most of the months of the year major part of agricultural labour and others engaged in allied activities are without continuous employment. There is continuous flow of rural-urban migration.

In urban areas there are mainly two types of unemployment; unemployment among industrial labourers and unemployment among educated middle class families. Urban unemployment is a reflection of rural poverty and unemployment and rural-urban migration. Thus, the surplus labour siphoned off the agricultural sector mainly comprise this type of urban unemployment.

Profs. Dandekar and Rath have opined in their study on the "Problem of Poverty in India", that urban poverty is only on outflow of rural poverty and as such for its eradication programmes to uplift the rural unemployed and underemployed will have to be initiated.

The committee on unemployment[20] also opined that urban unemployment is an outflow of rural unemployment and under-employment and therefore gainful rural employment programmes would reduce the influx of such persons to urban areas and thereby mitigate the acuteness of this type of urban unemployment. The tendency to migrate increases with the acquisition of educational qualifications. Educational status is a marketable commodity. Hence, schooling is used specifically to gain better employment for the child and the location of such employment usually entails migration.[21] ILO experts have the same opinion. They observed that migration from rural to urban areas have brought the problem of unemployment into sharper focus.[22]

6. MEASUREMENT OF UNEMPLOYMENT

Loss of manpower is one general criterion for measurement of unemployment. Unemployment can show the number of idle and wasteful hours, days or months due to lacking of proper work. It is loss of potential output due to lack of proper work. In this context we can refer four important criteria for measuring unemployment, namely, time criterion, income criterion, productivity criterion and willingness criterion. Let us explain these in short.

1. Time Approach. The time criterion is very important and useful for measure an unemployment. N.S.S. and many other organisations and researchers used the time criterion for measuring unemployment.

Unemployment means loss of productive time and for this loss of potential production. In loss of potential production and potential income this waste of time is most important factor. N.S.S. has adopted different time criterion in various rounds of researches. He used different reference period in different rounds. The reference day, reference week or reference year is the one preceding the day of enquiry. The reference period of the 9th N.S.S. round was one year and in 10th it was one day.

According to NSS data, persons having some gainful work however nominal on the reference day for at least one day in the reference week have been classified as employed; persons without gainful work throughout the reference period and seeking work or not seeking but available for work during the reference period or any one of the seven days of the reference week have been classified as unemployed.

In rural areas there is seasonal employment and unemployment. Therefore, we cannot classify these people into a rank of either employed or unemployed person. In this NSS method is very useful. According to this method, the information data of number of working hours in a week is collected. Using the information on hours at work and availability for additional work, NSS classified a person as underemployed if he worked below a certain normal number of hours during the week and reports availability for additional work. According to norms applied by the NSS in various rounds of studies 43-56 hours in week or 6-8 hours in a day is considered as a full employment. A person working 28 hours or less during the reference week and reporting availability for additional work has been treated as severely underemployed. Same way a person working 29 to 42 hours a week and reporting availability for additional work has been treated as moderately underemployed.

Planning Commission Approach. In each and every draft of five year plan, there is estimates of the backlog of unemployment at the beginning of the each plan and the likely additions to the labour force during the plan periods. These estimates were desired by (a) the employment potential of investment and growth in output during the plan period and (b) the information from the various rounds of the NSS and the employment exchange data with proper adjustment.

The Planning Commission has adopted four following norms in successive plans for calculating the number of unemployed people at the end of each plan :

(i) The number of persons unemployed at the beginning of the plan.

(ii) The net addition to the labour force during the plan period.

(iii) The number of jobs likely to be generated through the implementation of the plan as formulated.

(iv) Achievements in terms of employment on the basis of actual plan performance.

There is a limitation in the method of calculating rural unemployment because it ignored the visible or seasonal underemployment. In this context Dantwala Committee very rightly observed, "The agricultural workers other than wage labourers were wholly excluded." Thus, it was implicitly assumed that the problem of unemployment did not affect the self-employed in the rural population.

The Planning Commission presented for the first three plans, the estimates of the backlog of unemployment growth in labour force additional employment created and the backlog left behind during each successive plan period. The Planning Commission discontinued the estimates from the fourth plan onwards on the advice of the Dantwala Committee for the solution to be sought is in presenting a set of figures reflecting different aspects of unemployment and not in scraping, whatever figure one has, the alternative should be multi-dimensional approach rather than a zero dimensional approach. In this context noble prize winner Prof. A.K. Sen and Rajkrishna very rightly observed, "If the phenomenon of unemployment in an economy is too heterogeneous to justify aggregation into single dimensional magnitude the committee could have presented estimates based on alternative criteria."

2. Income Criterion. There is minimum income requirement of livelihood. If a person earns less income than that minimum income level, is considered to be unemployed. Thus, low income is proper measurement for unemployment and underemployment. Thus, the population below poverty line can be considered as a unemployed or underemployed.

Prof. Dandekar and Rath argued that an adequate level of employment must be defined in terns of providing minimum livelihood to the population. Earning of income is more important than the time or hours devoted to work. Dandekar and Rath observed, "An adequate level of employment must be defined in terms of its capacity to provide minimum living to the population."[23]

Underemployment is a basic cause for poverty. But the magnitude of poverty is greater than that of unemployment. It is a controversial issue at debate whether poverty directly associated with unemployment or not. In this context late Dr. D.T. Lakdawala observed, "In many poor regions of the country, unemployment rates are comparatively low... low standard of living of landless labourers are associated with fairly low unemployment rates."

3. Productivity Criterion. When labourers marginal productivity is less than some normal standard he is considered to be unemployed. This is very useful and accurate criterion for measuring disguised unemployment. Prof. Ragnar Nurkse defined disguised unemployment in the context of zero marginal productivity.[24] But here main problem is to measure the marginal productivity. Production is a joint efforts of all factors of production. In this context we are not to able to marginal productivity of single labourer.

4. Willingness Criterion. A person considered unemployer if he is willing to do more work than he is actually doing in present. A person who fail to obtain work even though he is willing to work should be regarded as unemployed. This type of unemployment is included in a category to a situation in which person's involuntary failure to get work, even though he is eagerly willing to do work.

Persons who are idle and not available for work should be excluded from the category of the unemployed or underemployed. In this context Prof. Harberger[25] observed that in every developing economy there are two sectors : an unprotected sector in the labour market and a sector protected by collective bargaining. The wages are very high in the protected sector. There is involuntary unemployment among the workers while they are on the look out for jobs in the protected sector. They opt for working in the unprotected sector only when they fail to get a job in the protected sector or when they do not get financial help from their people.

But S.S. Reddy[26] contends that this logic is not applicable in India. When a person tries to get a job in protected sector he will do so with minimum required qualification. Due to social status he is not willing to work in unprotected sector. Our people like to work or give top preference to work in the protected organised public or private sector even though last cadre also.

These are the four criterions for measuring unemployment. These are not separate or quite independent but complement to each other. Therefore, it is very difficult if not impossible to measure an unemployment from single criterion, integrated approach is needed for measuring unemployment.

7. ESTIMATES OF UNEMPLOYMENT

Our pattern of industrialisation has not increased employment opportunities properly due to capital intensive production method. Many studies have concluded that capital output ratio has increased. A study by Bhatia (1990)[27] concluded that capital output ratios was 2.22:1 during the first plan and it was 4.74 : 1 in the four years of the fifth plan. This shows the rising proportion of plan expenditure on capital intensive projects *vis-a-vis* labour intensive projects. Before this, Mathur (1980)[28] and Brahmananda (1980)[29] have concluded same facts. This also reflected that the measures to promote employment through special employment programmes and expansion of public sector employment yielded poor results.

The studies of Ghosh (1992)[30], Rangrajan (1997)[31] and Sharma (1970)[32] concluded that over the period 1972-73, 1987-88 employment elasticities with respect to growth have substantially declined. This is reflected in following table.

TABLE 1

Employment Elasticities

Sectors	Elasticity co-efficient			
	1973-74	1978-83	1983-88	1988-94
1. Agriculture	0.54	0.49	0.36	0.52
2. Mining Quarrying	0.95	0.67	0.85	1.05
3. Manufacturing	1.05	0.68	0.42	0.50
4. Construction	0.35	1.00	1.00	Neg.
5. Electricity, Gas and Water Supply	1.67	0.74	0.48	0.35
6. Transport, Storage and Communication	0.76	0.92	0.35	0.67
7. Services	0.80	0.99	0.42	0.87
All sectors	0.61	0.55	0.38	0.41

Notes : Based on Ghosh (1992), Rangrajan (1992) and Sharma (1997).

We give topmost priority to capital intensive industries. Therefore, mega industries have developed rapidly. Actually there is need of developed small scale industries which is employment-oriented. There is a growth of SSI. But it is not proper and perfect. Growth of SSI can be seen from the Table No. 2.

TABLE 2

Growth of SSI

Year	Total employ (in lakhs)	Total estb. (in lakhs)	Ave. emp. (No's)	Ave. prod. (Rs.)
1973-74	39.7	4.10	9.54	13,000
1975-76	45.9	5.46	8.33	13,998
1980-81	71.0	8.74	8.12	15,361
1985-86	96.0	13.53	7.10	18,538

Year	Total employ (in lakhs)	Total estb. (in lakhs)	Ave. emp. (No's)	Ave. prod. (Rs.)
1986-87	101.4	14.62	6.93	19,908
1987-88	107.0	15.83	6.76	21,254
1988-89	113.0	17.12	6.60	22,721
1989-90	119.6	18.26	6.55	23,928
1990-91	125.3	19.50	6.41	25,067
1991-92	129.8	20.80	6.22	24,936
1992-93	134.1	22.40	6.00	28,270
1993-94 (provisional)	139.4	23.80	5.90	—
1994-95 (provisional)	146.6	25.70	5.70	—

Production per worker in 1970-71 prices.
Source : Based on *Handbook of Industrial Statistics.*

Here we can see that average employment per SSI unit has considerably decreased during the time of new economic reform.

Industrial sickness is one important reason for unemployment. Most of the sick units are SSI units. In March, 1993-94 there were total 258307 sick industries, out of this 256452 units are small scale units. Industrial sickness shown in Table No. 3.

TABLE. 3
Industrial Sickness

	Non-SSI units		SSI Units	
Year December	Number	Loan (O/s) Rs. (crore)	Number	Loan (O/s) Rs. (crore)
1980	409	1324	23149	306
1981	422	1479	25342	359
1982	444	1791	58551	569
1983	491	2014	58363	729
1984	545	2330	91450	880
1985	637	2980	117783	1068
1986	714	3287	145776	1306
1987	1119	2802	204255	1797
1988	1241	3564	240573	2141

March				
1989-90	1455	4539	218823	2427
1990-91	1461	5106	221472	2787
1991-92	1536	5787	245575	3100
1992-93	1867	7901	228176	3351
1993-94	1915	8152	256452	3601

Note : Loan O/s is loan outstanding.

Source : CMIE, India's Industrial Sector, January 1996, Table 60, p. 62.

This table reflects the very serious problem of industrial sickness. In the sick industries, most of the units are small scale units. Sickness in SSI sector resulted in huge unemployment because as we know that this sector is employment-oriented sector. Outstanding loan is less in SSI sector compared to Non-SSI sector. But loss of employment is very high in sick SSI.

8. NEW ECONOMIC POLICY, LABOUR MARKET AND ITS PROBLEMS

After 1991, Government has adopted new economic policy, in which steps have been taken in reference to liberalization, privatization and globalization. Government has decreased its functions and has paid special attention towards stability of inflation and monetary matters. Efforts have been made to remove license system. Due to fundamental changes in economic policies, Indian labour market has been effected which has created some human problems. Similarly, fundamental change in labour market is recommended to get success in the steps taken under new economic policy.

1. Need of flexibility in labour market for fundamental changes. In reference to free economy, demand and supply factors should be working freely in labour market like any other market. Employment and wage laws and controls are hindrance here. Here wages are not fixed freely but they are fixed under the pressure of labour unions and control of government, so, wages cannot be attached with productivity or market condition. Demand and supply factors can freely work in labour market if this obstacle is removed. Employer should have full freedom regarding workers. Similarly, wage must be fixed by market factors.

But above factors are obstacles in making labour market flexible and free. Labour market cannot be compared with other market because labour is not a commodity but it's a living thing. Human, social and moral matters are attached with labour market. For producer wage is a part of the production cost, but for workers it is the only means of maintaining life.

2. Effects of minimum wage and job security on employment. Many economists have produced studies on effect of minimum wage and employment institutions on employment. Some of the main and important conclusions of the studies are as under :

1. In 1991, J.S. Weens has written an article, "The might of labour market clearing" in the book, "Toward Social Adjustment"and Concluded that unwanted unemployment of the labour market can be removed by decrease in real wages.
2. In 1992, Richard Freeman has stated that in some nations minimum wages create grave effect on employment. Effective implementation is not being done in the nations where very low wage has been decided. In such condition less employment effect on minimum wage has been observed. In curiosities minimum wage law of America was implemented before 1980, due to which employment level decreased and unemployment increased.
3. In 1987, Padleb and Riverose studied minimum wage laws of Latin America. They said that minimum wages cause mix effect on employment. There shall not be major change in employment by the change in minimum wages.
4. International Labour Organisation studied minimum wage law — 1970 and 1980 of Latin America. It said that minimum wage will not create any adverse effect on employment. So, wage cannot relay on demand market factors. Similarly a worker cannot be retrenched without giving enough time and compensation. He must be given chance for alternative job. Efficiency is directly connected with high and secured wages and job security. Low and unstable wages and job insecurity decreases efficiency.

The concept of Labour Market Cleaning : Basically renowned economists produced this concept. Government controls create rigidity in labour market which causes unemployment. Unemployment increases if government imposes controls over labour market continuously, interferes in it and if there is job security and wage law is being implemented. But if there is no control or government interference in labour market, then labour market works freely and demand and supply factors freely doing wage fixation and employment. So, there would be no problem of scarcity of labour in labour market. This situation is known as labour market cleaning. Some economists believe that wage difference and unemployment are natural. This condition cannot be avoided. That is why this concept is considered to be more theoretical and less practical.

Flexibility of labour market depends on labour market cleaning, in which shortage of labour or unwanted unemployment is not observed which means legal or institutional controls which effect wage and employment are not observed :

5. In 1991, Falan and Lucas studied regarding Zimbabawe and said that standard of employment and wage structure has improved due to minimum wage.
6. Houseman said in his study of European nations in 1991 that chances of employments are damaged due to job security.
7. Lazear in 1990 employment has been effected in O.E.C.D. nations due to provisions of higher wage requirement. This effect is very large scale. In Spain during 1980 level of employment was improved when fixed time employment contract was implemented in the place of permanent employment contract.
8. Falan and Lucas have said that job security has inverse relation with proportion of employment, means proportion of employment decreases due to job security. This study was made after independence of Zimbabawe.
9. In context of India, economists have represented study, according to which employment decrease during 8O's was due to job security laws and controls. According to studies of Lucas of the year 1988, there was increase of 86 per cent in real wages between the year 1960-61 to 1979-80. So, rate of employment has decreased during 1981-82, compared to 1959-60.
10. According to report represented by Ishwar Ahulawaliya in 1992, the real wages increased upto 34 per cent between 1980-81 and 1985-86 and hence, employment was decreased. United Industrial Production sector's employment increased at the rate of 2.01 per cent during the spell of 1978-83, while there was decrease of 0.09 per cent between 1983-88.

3. Labour adjustment in Industrial Reorganisation. It is a legal provision that prior government consent is necessary while closing down the factory or retrenching the labourers. This provision was made in 1976. According to which if there are 300 or more labourers in a unit then, prior government consent is needed before retrenching labourers. In 1980 this provision was amended and it was implemented for the units where 100 or more labourers are employed. According to opinion of experts, this provision makes adverse effects on employment level. To escape from this provision some administrators close the unit and retrech labourers by showing reasons like power problems, shortage of raw materials etc. Mr. B.B. Patel has said in his study that 36,000 labourers became unemployed between 1983-88 due to shut-down of textile mills of Ahmedabad. Similar study was made for united private sectors at Kanpur by Mr. Singh. Here, 4,000 workers had become unemployed due to closing of mills, while a lakhs labourers had become unemployed due to closing down of factories.

Sudipto Mundale, A learned economist has said in his report in 1993 that in next 3 years there shall be decrease of 2.4 million people in private and public sectors.

Thus, due to closing down of industries and due to financial crises large number of labourers are becoming unemployed. Unemployment shall increase very much if labour market shall not made adjustment with the dimensions which are being added in industries, due to implementation of new economic policies.

4. New Economic policy and jobless development. A number of jobs shall decrease due to new economic policy. The strategy and development of new economic policy is capital-oriented and technology-oriented, by which it will be a jobless development even if there is improvement in production and growth. B.B. Bhattacharya and Arun Mishra has tried to find out an employment elasticity on the basis of census. They have tried to find out this by the figures of 1991 census.

Sector	Employment elasticity
The whole economy	0.45 per cent
Primary sector	0.74 per cent
Manufacture	0.19 per cent
Construction	1.12 per cent
Business	0.37 per cent
Communication and Storage	0.34 per cent
Service sector	0.65 per cent

It is clear from this figure that there is minimum employment elasticity while primary sector has been neglected in new economic policies in which there is maximum employment elasticity and on which maximum attention has been given for economic reforms. Rate of employment has decreased and rate of unemployment has increased during new economic reforms periods. According to official figures rate of increase in unemployment was 3.01 per cent in 1990-91; 4.7 per cent in 1991-92; 5.2 per cent in 1992-93 and it was 5.5 per cent in 1993-94. Thus, proportion of unemployment has increased during economic reforms. During this spell proportion of task force has become 3.8 millions from 3.36 millions.

REFERENCES

1. Jean Mouly, "Some Remarks on the Concept of Employment and Unemployment", *International Labour Review*, Vol. 105, No. 2, Feb. 1972, p. 155.
2. Joan Robinson, *Introduction to the Theory of Employment*, Macmillan and Co., 57, Martin Press, 1970, p. 2.

3. *Encyclopaedia of Social Sciences*, Macmillan Co., New York, Vol. XV, p. 147.
4. *Encyclopaedia Britannica.*
5. International Labour Organisation, "The International Standardisation of Labour Statistics, Studies and Reports", New Series No. 53, Geneva, 1959, pp. 44-48.
6. Banerjee, S., "Employment Policy and Economic Growth", *The Indian Journal of Labour Economics*, Vol. IX, October 1968, p. 18.
7. Richard, A. Lester, *Economics of Labour*, The Macmillan Co., New York, p. 542.
8. C.S.O., *Standards for Surveys on Labour Force : Employment and Unemployment*, Department of Statistics, New Delhi, Govt. of India, 1961, p. 83.
9. Hutchison, T.W., *A Review of Economic Doctrines, 1870-1929*, Oxford University Press, p. 404.
10. Saxena, R.C., *Unemployment in Labour Welfare and Social Welfare*, Jaiprakashnath Sons, Meerut, 1968.
11. Raj, K.N., "Trends in Rural Unemployment in India," An Analysis with Reference to Conceptual and Measurement Problems, *Economic and Political Weekly*, Vol. XI, No. 31-33, August, 1976, pp. 1281-92.
12. Nural Islam, "Concept and Measurement of Unemployment and Under-employment", *International Labour Reviews*, March 1964, pp. 240-252.
13. Rajkrishna, "Unemployment in India", *Economic and Political Weekly*, Vol. 8-9, March 1983.
14. Sen, A.K., "Surplus Labour in India, A Critique of Shoultz's Statistical Test", *Economic Journal*, March 1967, Vol. XVIII, pp. 154-61.
15. Harber, W. and Levinson, H.M., "Labour Relation and Productivity in Building Trade," *op. cit.*, 1956.
16. International Labour Organisation, *Building, Civil Engineering and Public Works Committee Report*, "Seasonal Unemployment in the Construction Industry", Report III, of the Third Session, 1952.
17. Sivaswamy, N.R., *Employment Potential of the Indian Industrial Sector*, Academic Publishers, p. 6.
18. Sen, Amartya, *Employment, Technology and Development*, Oxford University Press, p. 3.
19. *The Report of the Committee of Experts on Unemployment Estimates*, 1970, p. 25.
20. *The Report of the Committee of Unemployment*, Govt. of India, Delhi, 1973, p. 14.
21. Cornell, Dasgupta *et al.*, *Migration from Rural Areas*, Oxford University Press, p. 61.
22. I.L.O., *International Labour Reviews*, January, 1956, p. 75.
23. Dandekar and Rath, "Poverty in India," *Economic and Political Weekly*, 9th January, 1971.
24. Nurkse, R., *Problems of Capital Formation in Underdeveloped Countries*, 1953, p. 23.
25. Harberger, A.C., *On Measuring Social Opportunity Cost of Labour*, ILO, Geneva, 1970.
26. Reddy, S.S., *Measurement of Unemployment : A Survey*, Vishaleshan, March 1981.
27. Bhatia, B.M., "Growth, Structural Change and Employment", *IASSI Quarterly*, Vol. 19, No. 1 and 2, pp. 1-12, 1990.

28. Mathur, G., "The Employment and Unemployment", in D.N. Narayana, *et al.* (eds.), 1980.

29. Brahmananda, P.R., "The Employment Function in the Indian Economy", in D.N. Narayana, *et al.* (eds.), 1980.

30. Ghosh, A., *Planning in India : The Challenge for Nineties*, Sase Publications, New Delhi, 1992.

31. Rangrajan, C., "Contours of Eighth Plan", *Yojana*, May 31, pp. 4-10.

32. Sharma, Alakh, N., *Trends in the Structure and Pattern of Employment and Unemployment Growth*, Working Paper Series No. E/188/97.